CHRISTIAN EDUCATION

An
Introduction
to
Its
Scope

Edited by
Douglas J. Simpson

CHRISTIAN EDUCATION
An Introduction to Its Scope
Copyright © 1978
RANDALL HOUSE PUBLICATIONS
NASHVILLE, TENNESSEE 37217

PRINTED IN THE UNITED STATES OF AMERICA
ISBN:
0-89265-053-2

FOREWORD

Those of us who are concerned with and involved in Christian education too often find ourselves so immersed in day-to-day problems that we seem to have little opportunity to stand back from our work and attempt to see the totality of our own work, much less see how our particular task is related to the whole scope of Christian education. Thus, we frequently fail to see that the product of Christian education, *i.e.*, the Christian, is the result of many people, organizations, and institutions—not to mention the Spirit of God.

The essays in this volume were written expressly for the purpose of broadening our understanding of the field of Christian education or for helping us refocus our thinking in the realm. The initial idea for this volume came from Rufus Coffey, and he, as well as others, have made invaluable suggestions throughout its development. Special indebtedness must be acknowledged for the editorial direction provided by Ansel Smith, Clarence Hearron, Blaine Hughes, and Jack Williams.

The writers of the individual chapters, too, must be thanked for their interest and cooperation in making this volume available. With one exception, all of these men have been or are presently pastors; therefore, it is hoped that the contents of this volume will be relevant to the local church. On the other hand, six of the ten authors have been or currently are professors. Thus, the volume is designed to meet some of the needs of an introductory course in the field of Christian education.

A final word of appreciation is due to Mary Ruth Wisehart who spent considerable time on the mechanical details of the manuscripts, and to Joy Ketteman who painstakingly typed all of the manuscripts. No one person, however, is responsible for the specifics of thought reflected in the volume. Each essay is ultimately the responsibility of the individual writer.

Tennessee State University   D. J. S.
Nashville, Tennessee
1978

to

Rufus Coffey

whose

concern

for

the

entire

scope of Christian education

is

deeply

appreciated

TABLE OF CONTENTS

Chapter I

The Scope Of Christian Education

by Douglas J. Simpson

Introduction

It is, to a certain extent, inevitable that our thinking about the scope of Christian education will be based upon the situation with which we are most familiar. But if our thinking about the scope of Christian education is influenced by a limited situation, we easily may be guilty of neglecting some of the most important facets of God's work and of overemphasizing a few facets of His work. We may, for instance, think of the scope only in terms of the extent or the range of the *objectives* of Christian education. To think in this manner is surely important; however, there are other significant ways of thinking about the scope of Christian education.

What are those additional ways of thinking about the scope of Christian education? Well, we may be inclined to analyze the scope according to the *institutions* that are crucial to the fulfillment of the objectives we establish. Unfortunately, some of us think only in terms of the institutional ramifications of Christian education.

Other angles that afford us insight into the scope of Christian education include examining the concept in the light of *organizations, truth,* and *people.* Naturally, there are other ways—some no doubt with more to recommend themselves—of viewing the scope of Christian education; but for our purposes we will look at the scope of Christian education from these perspectives. At this juncture, our treatment will be in terms of an overview. In later chapters, some aspects of these same topics are analyzed more extensively.

Before we examine these topics, we need to give some attention to the *nature* of Christian education. In other words, we need to become clearer about the concept of Christian education itself. Our discussion will be intentionally limited since there is a sense in which the remainder of this volume reflects on this subject. Our immediate interests, then, lead us to comment briefly on the following topics: 1) the nature of Christian education, 2) the objectives of Christian education, 3) the institutions of Christian education, 4) the organizations of Christian education, 5) the truth of Christian education, 6) the people of Christian education, and 7) the system of Christian education.

The Nature of Christian Education

In most uses of the term, *education* is thought to be concerned with the formation of desirable dispositions. The formation of dispositions includes developing specific abilities, skills, beliefs, attitudes, habits, and traits. Being educated, of course, is inseparably related to the learning of particular bodies of knowledge.

If we listen carefully to some segments of the educational world, we hear that acquiring any one set of dispositions is as good as learning any other set. In practice, however, those who adhere to this position are inconsistent: They attempt to convince others of the importance of particular sets of beliefs, attitudes, and habits.

The Christian approach to education is open about its concern for a specific set of dispositions. The distinguishing feature of Christian education is that it seeks to further dispositions that will enhance a person's opportunity to live for the Lord Jesus Christ, to enjoy the good life He offers us in this age, and to make a living that is consistent with a Christian life-style. This stance automatically implies that Christian education is not concerned with dispositions that are contrary to Christianity except, perhaps, in diminishing their influence, understanding human behavior, and so forth.

Several additional ideas stem from this explanation of Christian education. First of all, Christian education is not Christian if it fails to begin with the cultivation of those dispositions that are crucial to a person's opportunity to live for Christ. Anyone who thinks seriously about this notion recognizes that some areas of understanding are more important than others in attaining this objective.

Secondly, it is manifest that this view of Christian education causes us to concentrate on developing Christian dispositions rather than on eliminating unchristian dispositions. Seeking to develop Christian dispositions naturally leads to the elimination of some undesirable dispositions. Conversely, seeking to discourage or eradicate undesirable dispositions does not necessarily lead to developing Christian ones. Still there will be times when a direct approach to unchristian dispositions will be better than an indirect one.

As a third observation, it appears that this understanding of Christian education values helping people live for Christ more than it does helping them become either educated people or trained for specific jobs. No trichotomy is implied in this position, and Christian educators are not justified in slighting educational and professional realms. Yet, there is the clear implication that one of these three considerations—teaching people to live for Christ—has top priority in Christian education. This priority is reflected throughout this volume.

The Objectives of Christian Education

Although an intelligent understanding of the objectives of Christian education is not a panacea for all educational problems, it is still a major component in being a successful Christian. Misunderstanding in this realm frequently stems from either an excessively limited view of the scope itself or from our failure to appreciate the fact that objectives are partly dependent upon the particular situation under consideration. Having a limited comprehension of the range of our objectives can be illustrated in connection with the local church. Take the case of the church that seeks to make certain that its members are praying, meditating, worshiping fasting, and fellowshipping as they ought. Unless this group of believers has perceptive and conscientious leaders, it can easily neglect teachings about service, evangelism, benevolence, and giving.

Seeing objectives as they relate to each situation is also important. A Christian college, to illustrate a problem in this sphere, has objectives that are quite different—when taken in their totality—from those of a local church. Certainly both a church and a college are interested in promoting prayer, study, worship, meditation, fellowship, service, evangelism, giving, and similar interests that lead to the development of well-balanced, enthusiastic, mature Christians.

On the other hand, the academic nature of a college will

cause it to be interested in a broader range of activities and objectives. Unlike the local church, the college is keenly interested in developing an understanding of and an appreciation for history, music, philosophy, art, literature, mathematics, logic, psychology, biology, and other disciplines. The college is—or at least ought to be—concerned with the cultivation of both mature believers and educated believers. The church is basically concerned with the former of these objectives while indirectly contributing to the latter.

Let us repeat our thought: The objectives of Christian education are partially determined by the situation being considered. This being the case, one person, organization, or institution ought not to be critical of another simply because the second is not living up to the expectations of the first. Criticism should be based upon such considerations as whether the objectives being pursued are appropriate, whether these objectives are being met, and whether additional objectives should be pursued.

This is surely an extremely important point to make about objectives. We can go further, however. The day-to-day demand of operating any organization or institution can hinder our seeing new objectives and keeping in mind old objectives. People who do not see the whole scope of objectives, whether old or developing ones, may leave much undone. Consequently, people who are vitally interested in doing all that they ought to be doing for Christ welcome the suggestions, observations, and criticisms of others who have different perspectives. As Solomon put it, "The heart of the prudent getteth knowledge; and the ear of the wise seeketh knowledge" (Proverbs 18:15).

In this volume, we have been concerned with illustrating some of the ways in which objectives are reflected in the Old and New Testaments as well as in a number of specific settings. Our fundamental emphasis is on how the major objectives of the church should be understood by the individual believer, Christian parents, the pastor, staff members, organizations of the church, and several different kinds of educational institutions. While much has been left unsaid, the material included will hopefully stimulate thinking about even broader facets of the scope of Christian education.

Before moving on to the next point, let us pause to note that it is important to see the entire scope of Christian objectives for at least four reasons. One reason is so we, as much as is possible, can understand all that needs to be accomplished. Another reason is so that people will know who is responsible for specific objectives. Third, we can avoid wasteful overlap if the whole range of objectives is kept in mind. Finally, it is easier to evaluate our work if we clearly perceive the whole task.

The Institutions of Christian Education

Some institutions, like much else in Christian education, are permanent whereas others are transitory. Obviously, both the church and the home fit into the former category while other institutions fit into the latter. Christianity can survive, perhaps even thrive, without some institutions, but it cannot do so without Christian homes and churches.

In the light of this permanent-temporal analysis, it seems that temporal institutions ought to be considered as *supporting institutions*. Churches and homes do not exist, for example, to support schools, hospitals, and so on. No doubt they do support them, but that is not their major purpose for existing. Instead, temporal institutions exist to support the objectives of the church, home, and society.

Let us pause for a moment to further examine this relationship. The home and the church may and often should develop and support institutions that further their interests. Yet, they ought not to allow themselves to be used or manipulated by other institutions into supporting objectives that they find insignificant, unchristian, or obsolete. Similarly, Christian institutions have a responsibility to carefully consider new and developing interests of Christian homes and churches.

In turn, leaders of Christian institutions need to be cognizant of the fact that they are guiding transitory institutions to promote the well-being of permanent ones. Temporal institutions are merely culturally relevant ways of assisting transcultural, permanent institutions.

Ideally, the relationship between institutions should be a complementary one. Churches, homes, schools, colleges, and hospitals can contribute to the success of each other. Reality, however, often illustrates something else. Churches weaken homes by assuming parental duties rather than properly training parents. Schools have similar faults. Colleges can make students so critical that even after graduation they do more harm to local churches than good. Any institution can ignore certain problems and hope that some other institution will solve them. Still we must maintain that if we are faithful in studying the Scriptures and in thinking, feeling, and acting in the light of them, our institutions will be assets to each other.

How can a harmonious, complementary relationship develop and continue? No completely definitive answer is possible at this point. Yet important to this relationship is the realization by each institution that *it is only one part of a whole.*

Institutions may be uniquely important and permanent, but they are still just parts of a larger picture. No one institution, permanent or transitory, is to overvalue itself and look askance at others. Much like the body Paul describes in 1 Corinthians 12, all institutions have significant functions. Is the church, therefore, the whole? What about the home? And what shall we say of the Christian school, hospital, seminary, retirement home, college, or orphanage?

The answers are all the same. Each is a part—a significant part but still just a part of the whole. When we keep abreast of our roles as parts of a whole, we can welcome the rise of new institutions without being threatened and even recognize that our own demise—if we are identified with transitory institutions—is wise if changes in society, the church, and the home no longer call for us.

Time never alters the need for Christian homes and churches although it does call for new emphases by both. But the scope of Christian education, institutionally speaking, will be influenced in other realms by time. We can weep over the death of a useless institution, oppose the development of a needed one, and initiate one that is ill-advised. We have many options in Christian education; therefore, the need of wisdom and open scrutiny is best in seeking change in this area.

We have already alluded to the diversity of Christian institutions and how their objectives are both similar and unique. Further treatment of these goals is discussed in later chapters; however, our analyses have been limited to three categories of institutions: the home, the church, and the school. The latter type is examined from the perspective of different kinds of schools.

The Organizations of Christian Education

Since organizations are largely like transitory educational institutions, we will devote just a few words to them. To amplify this thought a little, we may say that the temporal nature of most organizations means that they especially exist for the purpose of assisting permanent institutions. Many of the activities of organizations are again merely culturally relevant means of reaching objectives. The existence of an organization, assuming it is not antithetic to the Christian frame of reference, should be determined by its usefulness. When the criterion of usefulness is not present, no one should be expected to promote an organization. Indeed, promoting an organization at all should be skeptically approached since it is the objectives, not the organization, we wish to further.

When the aims of an organization are permanent, we must be careful not to leave them unattended if the organization is discarded or seriously altered. Organizations for boys, girls, youth, men, and women may—for a variety of reasons—become obsolete. But the objectives, *e.g.*, fellowship and study, still need attention. So new methods of furthering these aims will need to be devised or old, continued organization will need to incorporate them.

In looking at the scope of Christian education from this perspective, we need to see the whole scope for the same reasons it is advisable to see the entire scope from the viewpoints of objectives and institutions. With these reasons in mind, then, it is fundamental to the well-being of the Christian community that leaders be aware of the emphases, strengths, and weaknesses of denominational, nondenominational, and transdenominational organizations. The local church will be particularly interested in organizations that can assist it in a broad spectrum of affairs, such as camping, teacher training, missions, Sunday schools, and retreats. In this volume, we have concentrated on discussing organizations as they contribute to the success of a local group of believers.

The Truth of Christian Education

The implications of truth in the field of Christian education may be one of the most important ways of looking at the scope of Christian education; for, we profess a strong interest in all truth. This profession is reflected in the statement that "all truth is God's truth." This maxim suggests that since all truth belongs to God, then the Christian—as God's child—ought to be interested in all truth.

The practical implementation of this position provides a number of opportunities for disagreement. But the church as a local group of believers has not been the center of much controversy. The scope of truth for the church has essentially been conceived of as embracing the realm of Biblical truth. The church has not normally been thought of as being interested in the study of sociology, chemistry, literature, and so on. Instead, the writings of the Old and New Testaments have been our cardinal concern. Surely this is as it should be, because we worship, edify, fellowship, serve, meditate, pray, evangelize, and give in the light of the Scriptures. Our whole lives are oriented around God's revelation.

Oddly, perhaps, our stated interest in the whole of Scriptures is often far from our experience. Many of us understand only a few truths taught in the Scriptures. Our teaching, preaching, and studying of a narrow range of Biblical truths have seriously limited the scope of Christian education in this sphere. This limitation is detrimental within itself, but its influence extends to limiting our view of the objectives in Christian education, too. As a result, our overall view of the scope of Christian education may be seriously distorted.

Our theory of all truth being God's is fine, but we must be careful not to let it remain simply theory. Also, we ought to be certain not to misunderstand our own theory. Our position does not mean that we ignore the contributions of psychology and other fields about communicating Biblical truths. Nor does it suggest we are to be unaware of the relevance of history and literature in understanding the Scriptures. Indirectly and secondarily, the local church has long been interested in a large number of disciplines.

Is the situation the same with the home? Paradoxically, the home is directly concerned with a large number of disciplines. Parents are primarily responsible for the spiritual growth of their children, but they—if they are wise—are also concerned that their children learn history, mathematics, science, and other subjects.

Since the church has not been directly concerned with extrabiblical studies, parents may be in a precarious position. On the one hand, they may not be capable of assisting their children in learning how to sift through extrabiblical studies for truth and error. On the other hand, they need to be able to so help their children but have no one who is responsible for developing in them abilities which will enable them to do so.

In this dilemma, the solution has frequently been one of three types. Some people have responded by building Christian schools. This approach relieves parents of the pressure of responsibilities in this sphere but does not prepare them personally to cope with the problem. Christian schools should be supported by believers, but we ought not to simply ease our consciences by establishing them. Our consciences should drive us to prepare ourselves to guide our children in extrabiblical studies as well as in Biblical realms.

Other folks have basically ignored the problem and allowed things to go their natural way. The natural way usually includes their children gradually becoming partially, sometimes largely, conformed to the thinking of the world. These parents, like the parents who select the first option, may never become qualified to ensure that their children become educated Christians.

Another group of people have sought to get public schools to promote Christian truths and values. This plan can never be highly successful for a variety of reasons, but if it were successful, parents probably would still remain unqualified to help their children.

The inadequacy of all of these solutions may suggest that the church needs to rethink its direct involvement with extrabiblical areas of understanding. Perhaps the church ought to consider ways of helping both parents and youth in this realm.

Beyond the home and the church, the scope of truth in Christian education takes on different dimensions and orientations. A comment on Christian day schools and colleges will suffice to illustrate this point. By their very natures, these institutions have to be concerned with extrabiblical studies. They are involved with initiating students into different forms of knowledge, enabling students to evaluate these forms, and assisting students in the pursuit of new knowledge through appropriate kinds of research. These aims are impossible to reach in any idealistic sense. In a realistic sense, however, the scope of truth is later discussed in this volume. Picirilli gives attention to the scope of truth in connection with the major objectives of the church. Others, particularly O'Donnell, devote considerable attention to the scope of truth in other contexts.

The People of Christian Education

Regardless of which objective we are thinking about, it is improperly understood if it is not seen in connection with people. People, too, make up institutions and organizations. Similarly, truth is not intended to be seen as abstract ideas but as ideas that are pertinent to the people who understand them.

We must not, therefore, lose sight of the fact that people are more important than the programs, facilities, buildings, and materials we build or develop. People are not made to serve organizations, programs, and institutions anymore than they were made for the Sabbath. We are to serve God and each other by using a variety of methods, *e.g.*, organizations, programs, institutions.

Even our objectives need to be viewed as they relate to people. The nature and value of human beings must always be kept in focus when our objectives are stated, and we dare not seek to fulfill our objectives in a manner that is destructive to those who are created in the image of God.

We conclude, therefore, that people are of primary importance in Christian education. But how shall we conceive of people? What is the scope of Christian education as it relates to people? A popular method of examining this aspect of the scope of Christian education is to think in terms of age levels. This approach normally concentrates on seeing people as babies, children, youth, and adults. A less popular method is to think of the needs of people in terms of sex classifications. The scope may also be analyzed from a theological viewpoint, such as seeing people as pastors, deacons, and laymen. Recently we have had it called to our attention that the scope of Christian education includes people of all races whether nearby or in some distant country. The last part of our previous sentence, *whether nearby or in some distant country*, suggests a geographical way of looking at people. Then, too, we can think of people in terms of believers and unbelievers and as immature believers and maturing believers. Culturally speaking, the scope of Christian education includes people in all socioeconomic status groups. Psychologists might argue that we should see people as emotional, volitional, and intellectual beings.

These ways of looking at people enable us to better evaluate our emphases. We can determine, for example, if we are neglecting certain age levels. Likewise, we can decide if our churches are women-centered. Further, do we have a balanced emphasis on pastors, deacons, and laymen? Are we ministering to the different races in our community? Do we neglect some socioeconomic groups? Do we appeal to the whole person in our Christian education programs?

Naturally, there are other ways of viewing people. In this volume, we have concentrated on understanding the roles of people in Christian education as pastors, parents, church staff members, and individual believers. But our scope of understanding ought not to be limited by this approach.

The System of Christian Education

The term *system* is normally used to refer to a formal,

orderly arrangement of things. A highly developed system of Christian education demands the intentional arrangement of the various aspects of the field. We are not necessarily implying such an organization. Circumstances will influence how formal our system will be. What we are suggesting is that a "seeing of the whole," whether formally or informally connected, is important in the area of Christian education.

Ordinarily we are more accustomed to hearing of a system of Christian truth or systematic theology than we are a system of Christian education. Perhaps this lack of familiarity with the concept reveals one of our greatest weaknesses in the field of Christian education: a fragmented, disorganized, and blurred picture of God's workings among us. Our understanding of the scope of Christian education may be comparable to viewing scattered pieces of a puzzle.

This lack of coherent understanding affects our comprehension of both the parts and the whole of Christian education. Consequently, we need to work toward seeing the entirety of Christian education so we can appreciate, encourage, and, on occasion, participate in aspects of the overall task that we are not involved in on an everyday basis. Hopefully, we take a step in this direction in this volume. In part, what we wish to do is assist individuals and groups of believers in understanding the whole scope of Christian education. Another emphasis is to encourage involvement in some aspects of the scope of Christian education. Our understanding of the scope of Christian education as presented in this volume may be aided by the following diagram:

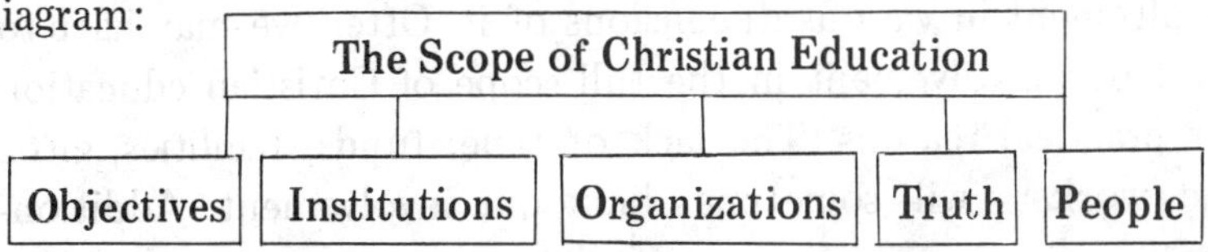

The Scope of Christian Education				
Objectives	Institutions	Organizations	Truth	People

This diagram, then, refers to both the scope of Christian education and a systematic way of viewing Christian education. Naturally, each of these major aspects of the scope of Christian education has subcategories that need to be considered. In future chapters, we deal with the various aspects of Christian education in a number of ways. In chapter IV we devote special attention to the objectives of Christian education but do not limit our discussion of them to this chapter. Chapter X concentrates on Christian institutions but chapters VI, VII, VIII, and IX have a direct bearing on the home and the church. Only one chapter, IX, is designed to analyze organizations, but there are organizational principles scattered throughout our discussions. The scope of truth in Christian education is treated from a Biblical perspective in chapters II, III, and IV with a sprinkling of comments in other chapters. The people of Christian education are stressed in chapters V, VI, VII, VIII, and XI. No chapter, of course, totally ignores this subject. Each chapter, we must remember, is concerned with some aspect of the scope of Christian education. As a result, we need to be alert to the implications of such.

Conclusion

The scope of Christian education is a multifarious subject. We are well-advised to understand the broad implications of the concept so that we may more effectively evaluate our own involvement in various dimensions of it. Often we may have to limit our involvement in the full scope of Christian education for practical reasons. The lack of time, funds, facilities, gifts, and workers will sometimes limit our involvement. Additionally, the leadership of the Spirit will have to be taken into consideration. No one person, therefore, can become deeply involved in all aspects of the total scope of Christian education. A church, however, can become more involved. Groups of churches may become even more deeply involved.

When we limit our involvement in some facets of Christian education, the reasons for our limited involvement ought to be sound. That is to say, we must be careful not to limit our involvement because of ignorance, lack of compassion, prejudice, indifference, or other motives that are hindrances to the cause of Christ.

Discussion Questions

1. The author says there are additional ways of viewing the scope of Christian education. What do you think he has in mind?
2. Has the author overstated his case when he says, "Christian education values helping people live for Christ more than it does helping them become either educated people or trained for specific jobs"? State the reasons for your answer.
3. What do you think the author means by enjoying the "good life He (Christ) offers us in this age"? How would you think the good life is developed?
4. Consider your own understanding of Christian education. Have you been oriented toward an unbalanced picture of the field? What facets of Christian education do you feel have been overemphasized and underemphasized? What accounts for these unbalanced emphases?
5. Summarize the author's reasons for suggesting we need to see the whole of Christian education. Are his reasons well founded?

6. We are told, "People who do not see the whole scope of objectives, whether old or developing ones, may leave much undone." Is this so?

7. Can you refute the author's assertion that "seeking to develop Christian dispositions naturally leads to the elimination of some undesirable dispositions"? Is he basically making a claim that as the fruit of the Spirit is cultivated the works of the flesh gradually disappear?

8. Is the author's analogy correct when he says, "People are not made to serve organizations, programs, and institutions any more than they were made for the Sabbath"? Support your answer.

Chapter II

Jewish Educational Practices

by Ralph Hampton

Introduction

We have seen in the previous chapter that one way of looking at the scope of Christian education is from the perspective of truth. Now our attention is turned to one aspect of truth: the Old Testament. In a slightly broader sense, we are interested in Jewish educational practices as the forerunner and the foundation of Christian education.

The reason for our interest in Jewish educational practices is that Christian education has its historical and theological roots deeply and firmly embedded in time. Just as the revelation of the New Testament builds upon that of the Old Testament, so the educational principles and practices of New Testament Christianity are best understood in light of Israel's educational history. Clarence Benson notes that the New Testament program of education introduced by Christ and practiced by the early church was only an enlargement and an improvement of the Old Testament plan.[1] All true religious education is grounded in the self-revelation of God. He is both the Teacher and the Truth to be learned. God, however, has used both heavenly and earthly instruments in His program of education for His people. In studying the educational practices employed among the people of Israel, we actually will be examining the educational program of God as He developed it among His chosen people—at least to the extent that Israel's practices conformed to God's plan.

The curriculum for religious education has been provided

by means of Divine revelation. The content of the curriculum is the truth about God, about man, about sin, about redemption, and about God's perfect plan for people. God's purpose is redemptive. He designed to bring His chosen people to a personal knowledge of Himself as Creator and Redeemer in a covenant relationship of fellowship. As a necessary element in that purpose, God determined to make men righteous, both in legal standing before Him and in practice. Moreover, Israel was chosen to be the instrument of God's redemptive grace to all the nations of the world. In different periods of Old Testament history, God employed various means of instruction. The content of the instruction was progressive as revelation became fuller. The ultimate goals remained unchanged. Christianity is the climax of God's redemptive program.

From Adam to Moses

To understand Jewish educational practices, we must trace their origins back to the very beginnings of God's dealing with man. Though many basic elements of God's program are unchanging, there have been continuing developments in that program. *In the beginning, God dealt personally and directly with men.* He personally instructed Adam and personally confronted Cain the murderer, for example. God continued to use this method but with ever decreasing frequency and only with select individuals.

At the very outset, God instructed Adam as to his duties. Adam was charged with the dressing of the garden (Genesis 2:15). He was assigned dominion over the creation and commanded to multiply and fill the earth (Genesis 1:28). The

Lord instructed Adam concerning what he was to eat and not eat. He was warned particularly not to eat of the fruit of the tree of the knowledge of good and evil (Genesis 1:29; 2:16, 17). At that point, Adam's moral-religious education began. In spite of the fact that he had the only perfect Teacher, Adam rejected the commandment of God and sought an experiential knowledge of good and evil. Thus began the conflict between the wisdom of God and the Satanic wisdom of this world, a conflict that continues to bring confusion and strife in the realm of education.

After Adam's fall into sin, God revealed the consequences to him and his wife. He provided an object lesson for them by providing a coat of skins to hide their nakedness as a replacement of their own inadequate covering of fig leaves. Nothing is recorded of God's further dealings with Adam. No mention is made of sacrifice. Yet, it seems reasonable to assume that some instruction was given in that matter. Genesis 4 records the sons of Adam, Cain and Abel, offering sacrifices to God. Apparently they were instructed by their father and by his example. Cain's sin at this point was not a matter of ignorance but of heart attitude.

Though God spoke personally to individual men throughout the early stages of human history, *it appears that from the very first His plan was to work through the head of the family.* The family was the first institution God established among men. Little detail is given, but it is recorded that men began to call upon the Lord when Seth had a family (Genesis 4:26). That godly family included Enoch who had a special relationship with God. When the human race became so corrupt that God determined to bring judgment upon the earth, He chose Noah and his family. After the flood God ordained a system of human government through which He would fulfill His purpose (Genesis 9:5, 6).   Mankind's rebelliousness led to further judgment by God at Babel where the race was divided (Genesis 11:1-9). God's program became clearer with the call of Abraham. He was chosen to be the father of a nation, to head a vast posterity of individuals who would walk in God's ways.

We learn from the traditions recorded by Josephus that Abraham was a highly educated man, a teacher of men. He was said to be skilled in "celestial science," a man of great wisdom and understanding. In fact, he was reported to have introduced arithmetic and astronomy to the Egyptians.[2] Abraham was certainly chosen by God for a ministry of teaching whether these traditions are true or not. God said of Abraham, "For I know him, that he will command his children and his household after him, and they shall keep the way of the LORD, to do justice and judgment; that the LORD may bring upon Abraham that which he hath spoken of him" (Genesis 18:19). The true sense of the verse is that God chose Abraham in order that he might teach his household God's ways. Godly Isaac is ample proof that Abraham did fulfill God's purpose in this matter. Obviously Abraham was the teacher of the entire household. His servant Eliezer is seen to be a most devout man. Abraham taught his household in other matters also. When Lot was captured by invaders from Mesopotamia, Abraham rescued him with a band of 318 servants who were born in his household and trained, presumably by Abraham (Genesis 14:14).

Thus from the beginning, education among the Hebrews was centered in the family. The patriarch was the teacher and priest of his household. Even when Israel had more formal programs of education and a priesthood to teach God's Word, the basic unit of education continued to be the family. From their birth, the Hebrew mother spoke to her babies of God and His marvelous works. The daughters were later instructed in the domestic skills by their mother. Except for the years at his mother's knee, the Hebrew boy received most of his training from his father. Throughout childhood the ways of the Lord and His covenant promises to Abraham were brought before the boy. As his sister learned domestic skills, so the son learned the necessary skills of living. Vocational training was never separated from religious training. All of life was recognized to be sacred. Whether it was Isaac digging wells (Genesis 26:22) or Jacob tending cattle for Laban (Genesis 31:9), the patriarchs saw God's hand at work in their daily lives.

From Moses to the Babylonian Exile

If we study carefully the Old Testament Scriptures, we will see that the heart of the educational program of the patriarchs was God's covenant with Abraham. Though Abraham surely told it to Isaac and Isaac to Jacob, the Lord Himself confirmed the covenant with each of the patriarchs. Through the family unit, the ways of the Lord were passed from generation to generation. Even 430 years in Egypt, with all the adverse effects that produced, did not obliterate the knowledge of the Lord among the sons of Jacob. In their distress, they cried out, and God had respect to their cries. There was faith among them, as in the case of Moses' parents who defied the king and saved their son (Hebrews 11:23).

God raised up Moses to deliver the Hebrews from the bondage of Egypt. *Moses was chosen not merely as a deliverer for the Hebrews, but—as we shall soon see—he was also chosen to become the greatest religious educator in history. He was given the responsibility to teach a whole nation the ways of the Lord.* Men, women, children, and even servants were included. Moses was prepared for his role by a background in all the learning of Egypt, forty years of discipline in the wilderness of Midian, and finally by direct revelation from God at Mt. Sinai.

Moses launched the first national, compulsory educational program in history at the command of the Lord. The curriculum was delivered to Moses from heaven. Though it was the most complete revelation of God's will given to date, the purpose was unchanged. Men and women were to fear God and keep His commandments. *Though the law of Moses provided for a priesthood, the basic responsibility for education remained with the family.*

The entire sixth chapter of Deuteronomy is a charge to faithful obedience in this matter. The heart of the Divine program is expressed in these words, "And thou shalt teach them diligently unto thy children, and shalt talk of them when thou sittest in thine house, and when thou walkest by the way, and when thou liest down, and when thou risest up" (Deuteronomy 6:7). The Hebrews took literally the commandments in Deuteronomy 6:8, 9. They fastened portions of the Law to the doorposts of the house and wore them upon their wrists and foreheads. A daily, constant reminder of God's Law and the need to obey it was thus emphasized.

In later times, the psalmist echoed the Divine imperative, "For he established a testimony in Jacob, and appointed a law in Israel, which he commanded our fathers, that they should make them known to their children: That the generation to come might know them, even the children which should be born; who should arise and declare them to their children"

(Psalm 78: 5, 6). At its best, the family was an outstanding means of religious instruction. The teaching was largely informal, always personal, and involved the learners in a real life activity. Faithful teaching of the Law and the history of Israel in the family produced some of Israel's greatest men and women and elevated the nation to a place of greatness.

The Law itself was an instructor. It set forth the demands of God upon His people. Right and wrong were clearly marked off by this revealed truth. Man's sinfulness and God's holiness were placed in sharp contrast through the commandments of the Lord. The Law did more, however. It also mapped out a daily way of life for all who received it to walk in its precepts. God's law dealt not only with moral issues, but it also provided instructions in matters of religious ritual and the everyday affairs of life. Diet, clothing, property, work, politics, and religion were all included in its prescriptions.

God assigned the priests a special responsibility to teach the Law. Obviously, each new generation of the sons of Aaron would need to be instructed in the duties of the priesthood as well as the other laws of God. All the people had to be instructed in the rituals of worship and the required sacrifices (Leviticus 10:8-11; Deuteronomy 33:10). Once each seven years in the sabbatical year during the Feast of Tabernacles, the priests were commanded to read the law of Moses to the assembled people so that they might *hear* the law, and *learn*, and *fear* the *Lord* and *observe* His commandments (Deuteronomy 31:10-13). Knowledge without obedience was never the goal.

The tabernacle-temple ritual and the sacrificial system provided a living, dramatic presentation of Divine truth. It was an educational experience in which the worshiper was a participant as well as an observer. The very construction of the sanctuary emphasized that access to a holy God was possible only through a priest and only by atonement for sin. Israel was constantly reminded that sin separates from God and that access to God is only upon His conditions. Whether one was seeking pardon for sin or coming to offer praises, a sacrifice was necessary.

One of God's most unique teaching tools was the use of the various religious festivals. The Scriptures tell us that some lasted as long as a week. All were dramatic and exciting. These festivals recalled Israel's history and God's past workings with the nation. Passover, for example, recalled the deliverance from the tenth plague when the death angel passed over the houses of the Hebrews where the blood of the lamb was sprinkled. It also reminded them of the escape from Egypt. Even the children participated in the celebration of these feasts. The Passover was eaten by one or more families. At the Passover meal the youngest son inquired of his father what this all meant, thus affording opportunity to retell the story of God's deliverance (Exodus 12:26, 27).

The duty of the fathers to recall Israel's history and God's deliverance was specifically commanded (Deuteronomy 6:20-25). Each of the great festivals contributed to Israel's religious education. Tabernacles recalled the years of wilderness wanderings when God preserved and provided for His people. Not only was the story retold each year, but it was also relived when the people moved out of their houses into temporary booths for a week. The festival of Purim celebrated the deliverance of the Jews from Haman's plot in the days of Esther. The celebration of Purim was thus a lesson in history and God's redemptive mercy and grace.

The effect of these festivals and others was undoubtedly very impressive, especially for the young. Faithful observance of the Divinely appointed festivals would have done much to keep the people true to God. They had great educational value. As J. M. Price observes: they were objective—appealing to all the various senses—they involved the learner in activity; they were dramatic; and they were often intensive, some lasting for several days.[3]

The Laws of the Lord and the works of God were thus presented in many different ways. *Music played a large part in worship and instruction.* Israel's history and God's deliverance were often proclaimed in psalm (see Exodus 15:1-21; Deuteronomy 31:19-22; Psalm 78). Even the placing of stone monuments served as opportunities for religious instruction (Joshua 4:5-7). On every side the Hebrews were confronted with reminders of the Law of the Lord and the Lord's faithfulness to Israel. Religious education was never divorced from daily life.

In spite of the fact that God ordained a full-orbed program of religious instruction that involved parents, priests, public instruction, and public worship, Israel continued to manifest propensities toward backsliding. Even the priests turned away from the Lord at times. God raised up prophets to instruct His people in the true paths of righteousness and to call the people back to a new obedience. In addition to idolatry, one of the problems the prophets faced was that of a formal, insincere religious observance (see Isaiah 1:11-18).

God was not without His prophets from Moses to Malachi, but in the darkest days of Israel's history, He raised up some of His choice servants. Elijah and Elisha confronted the perils of Baalism when it seemed that hell would exterminate the true worship of the Lord. In the declining days of the divided kingdoms from the eighth century B.C. onward through the exile and to the return of the remnant, God gave His people great prophets. In the sinful days before the exile there were men like Amos, Hosea, Micah, Isaiah, and Jeremiah. During the exile there were the ministries of Jeremiah, Ezekiel, and Daniel. After the exile, God exhorted and comforted His people through such men as Haggai, Zechariah, and Malachi.

The prophets were the greatest moral and religious teachers of ancient Israel. They proclaimed the true character of God. His holy, righteous character was set in contrast with the wickedness of the day. These fearless men of God spoke of coming judgment and then of a brighter day for Israel. They demonstrated that the God of Israel is Lord of all the earth, the God who controls history. It is of special importance that they predicted the coming of Messiah and a glorious future for God's people.

In addition to the prophets named in Scripture, there are many "nameless" men of God. Mention is made of the "company of the prophets" in connection with Samuel (1 Samuel 10:5; 19:20) and the "sons of the prophets" in connection with Elijah (2 Kings 2:3) and Elisha (2 Kings 6:1). The exact ministry of these men is uncertain. It has been suggested that they were trained by the famous prophets with whom they were associated. Having been trained, they then are thought to have helped spread the message of the prophet who trained them.

Yet another group of men who were teachers of Israel were the "wise men." Wise men were found among all the great nations of antiquity, including Israel. These wise men wrote and compiled the wisdom of their day. Solomon was both a writer and a compiler of wisdom literature. The wise men provided practical axiomatic truths for dealing with life's problems. Their teachings promoted righteousness. The book of Proverbs is a collection of such teachings designed especially for the instruction of the young (Proverbs 1:1-8). The purpose of the Proverbs is to instruct the young in that wisdom which has the fear of the Lord as its heart. The wisdom of Solomon is summed up in Ecclesiastes 12:13, "Let us hear the conclusion of the whole matter: Fear God, and keep his commandments: for this is the whole duty of man."

In God's plan of religious instruction for Israel, the political leaders had a vital role. Men like Moses, Joshua, and Samuel were both political and spiritual leaders. Moses, of course, was the instructor of all his people. He even taught the priests the Law of God. Joshua erected a stone monument at the Jordan as an educational device to aid future generations to recall the works of God (Joshua 4:5-7). At Mt. Ebal, Joshua wrote a copy of the Law upon stones. With the congregation of Israel divided upon Mt. Ebal and Mt. Gerizim, Joshua caused the Law to be read in the presence of all the people (Joshua 8:32-35). Such public readings were certainly quite impressive.

During the monarchy, devout kings made a significant contribution. In particular, we see that David made a notable contribution to the religious education of Israel through his Psalms which instruct as well as provide an expression of devotion for worship. Solomon wrote some psalms, but his chief role as a teacher was a wise man. His greatest contribution was the writing and collection of Proverbs. Unfortunately, he did not practice the wisdom of the Lord in his own life.

Those reform kings of Judah who endeavoured to bring about revival in their land were active in the promotion of religious education. One of the most striking examples is the case of Jehoshaphat. He earnestly sought to eradicate idolatry in Judah and to revive the worship of the Lord. To achieve this latter end, Jehoshaphat sent out princes, Levites, and priests to teach the law of the Lord to the people in the various cities of Judah (2 Chronicles 17:6-9). A considerable revival in the land resulted from this undertaking.

Another king who led in a major spiritual renewal was Hezekiah. Under his leadership, one of the greatest Passover celebrations in history was kept. In addition to cleansing the temple and restoring regular worship after the idolatry of Ahaz, Hezekiah sent his messengers into the northern tribes to invite people to assemble for the Passover celebration. Hezekiah also exhorted the people to be faithful to support the priests and Levites (2 Chronicles 29-31). He encouraged the teaching ministry of the Levites according to 2 Chronicles 30:22.

The last godly king of Judah, Josiah, also led his people in a religious renewal based upon instruction in the Law of the Lord. Josiah was greatly moved by the sin of his people when he first heard the Law read. Not only did he mourn for the sins of the nation, he had the priests, the Levites, the elders of the people, and the inhabitants of Jerusalem assembled for a public reading of the words of the Law. After the Law was read, he led the people in a renewal of their covenant with the Lord (2 Chronicles 34:29-32). He also gave encouragement to the priests and Levites in their work (2 Chronicles 35:2, 3). In the theocracy, it was clearly the king's duty to see after the spiritual and moral welfare of his people. The king was commanded to make himself a copy of the Law. He was to read it, fear God, and obey His commandments all the days of his life (Deuteronomy 17:18-20). The record indicates, however, that only a few of Judah's kings and none of those in the northern kingdom of

Israel were faithful to their spiritual responsibility.

In spite of the many means God provided for the religious instruction of His people, it is sad to find that the nation turned away from His truth to the lie of idolatry. They looked to false prophets and other gods. There was a failure of religious education at every level. Fathers, priests, and prophets were all represented among the apostates in the land. Those responsible for Israel's religious instruction helped to pervert her (Isaiah 9:14-16). Even the faithful prophets of the Lord were not able to turn the hearts of the people back to Him. The efforts of godly kings resulted only in partial and temporary revivals. First, Israel, then Judah fell before their powerful neighbors as God judged them for their failure to keep His commandments.

The downfall of these kingdoms was designed to teach the Jews to both teach and practice the Law of the Lord. Hosea wrote of Israel, "My people are destroyed for lack of knowledge: because thou has rejected knowledge, I will also reject thee ... " (Hosea 4:6). We find the same thought expressed by Jeremiah concerning his nation of Judah, "For my people is foolish, they have not known me; they are sottish children, and they have none understanding: they are wise to do evil, but to do good they have no knowledge" (Jeremiah 4:22). Isaiah declared of Judah, "Therefore my people are gone into captivity, because they have no knowledge" (Isaiah 5:13). This does not mean that they did not know anything about God or His Law. The problem was that there was no real knowledge of God. They did not know Him. They did not obey Him or love Him.

Discipline was an element in the progess of education God prescribed for His people. Parents were not to spare the rod in the discipline of their children (Proverbs 22:15; 23:13, 14). In like manner,God dealt with the people as a whole. He gave them the positive instruction of His Word through their teachers. When the people refused His Word and rebelled, God disciplined them as a people. God used drought, famine, plagues of insects, and war to discipline His disobedient people. From time to time, He let their enemies subject them. When all else failed, God raised up the nations of Assyria and Chaldea to take His rebellious people into captivity that they might learn to obey His Law.

The Post Exilic Era

When Nebuchadnezzar's troops destroyed Jerusalem and the Temple and carried away most of the inhabitants, it looked like the end of the nation of Israel forever, humanly speaking. As we know, though, God had promised to restore a remnant. He had a covenant to keep with Abraham and David. In time a remnant did return from exile. Though there were still problems, it appears that those who returned had learned from the rigorous discipline of the Lord. Clarence Benson concludes that the exile taught the Jews at least three lessons. After that experience, they despised idolatry and drunkenness and the folly of neglecting religious instruction.[4] These three sins had brought about their downfall, particularly the neglect of instruction in God's Word.

Those Jews who returned to Jerusalem after their release by Cyrus showed a marked increase in their concern for religious instruction. *God raised up faithful men to lead in the education of the people.* The ministry of Ezra, the "ready scribe," is most notable in this connection. When he first arrived in Jerusalem,

Ezra saw that the people were guilty of certain sins, especially intermarriage with the heathen. After a prayer of confession and intercession he led the people to put away their heathen wives and renew the covenant with God (Ezra 9, 10).

Ezra was joined by Nehemiah in another major project to correct certain evils in Jerusalem several years later. On one occasion the people assembled in the street and requested Ezra to read them the Law of Moses. For a half a day, he read the Law as the people stood listening. Ezra was aided by certain Levites who helped the people to understand what the Law meant. In addition to explaining the Law, there was perhaps a problem in understanding Hebrew. Some of the people were by now using Aramaic. Nehemiah 8:8 describes the teaching ministry of Ezra and his aides: "So they read in the book in the law of God distinctly, and gave the sense, and caused them to understand the reading." The people were moved to tears by the Word of God. As a result they separated themselves from their sins and renewed the covenant.

During the exile, the Jews had no access to the temple. Regular worship and sacrifice were impossible. Considerable respect for the priesthood had been lost because of the failure of the priests to lead the nation in God's ways. *While in Babylon, the Jews developed a new religious institution. This institution was called the synagogue, an assembly of people meeting together to study the Law of God.* The synagogue was born out of practical necessity. It supplanted the temple as the place of teaching the Law. By the time of Jesus, synagogues were to be found wherever Jews were found in the Roman empire.

Of course the temple was rebuilt after the exile. Once again, it was the site of animal sacrifice and of worship.

However, the influence of the priests as Israel's religious teachers had declined seriously. *A new class of teachers had arisen in connection with the synagogue. They were scribes or rabbis.* They first became knowledgeable in the Word of God because they worked as scribes, making copies of the holy writings. In time, they became a well-qualified group of teachers of the Law. The Jews count Ezra to be the first rabbi. Some of the rabbis were also priests like Ezra, but one did not need to belong to any tribe or sect to become a rabbi. *The Law was taught in the synagogue in regular services on the Sabbath and on Mondays and Thursdays, which were market days, as well as on appointed holy days.* On each Sabbath the Law was read publicly twice and expounded upon. A portion was also read from the prophets at each service. The reading from the Law was so arranged that the Law was read completely in a three-year cycle. Jewish religious life centered around the synagogue, especially in cities and towns any distance from Jerusalem.

During the intertestamental period, elementary schools were introduced in connection with the synagogue. By the time of Christ there were reportedly 480 synagogue schools in Jerusalem alone. Though that number is highly questionable, it certainly indicates that there was a major educational thrust among the Jews. This is truly remarkable. From the earliest history the Hebrews had emphasized education, especially the teaching of the Law to the young. Yet, there had not been schools as such prior to this time. What caused this new emphasis on schools? Eby and Arrowood offer four possible causes: a) It was apparent that family education alone was inadequate to preserve the national culture and purity of worship; b) Acquaintance with the culture of Babylon showed the Jewish leaders the need for schools; c) Increased knowledge, including a growing body of oral learning, made more education essential; d) There was an increased demand for the ability to read and write due to demand for training in the written Law.[5] Behind all this was the desire to avert a repetition of the national calamity that led to the Babylonian captivity.

The elementary schools were for boys 5 or 6 to 10 years of age. Girls were not included until much later. Boys also received their first religious education at home. By the time they started to school, they had already memorized some passages of Scripture as well as hymns and prayers. The primary study in the elementary school was the Law, starting with Leviticus. Though the boys were taught to know the Law, the chief emphasis was upon *doing* or keeping its precepts. The basic method of teaching was memorization. Personal copies of the Law were not easily available in pre-printing press days. Thus, Jewish boys were required to memorize portions of the Old Testament, especially the Pentateuch. The students learned reading, writing, simple arithmetic, Jewish history, and geography from their one textbook.

The classroom procedures were well defined. The pupils usually sat upon the ground around their teacher. Skill in writing was first acquired with a stylus on a clay tablet. Later the pupils advanced to papyrus or parchment and a pen. Though the approach was definitely content centered, there was ample opportunity for expression. The students recited their lessons orally. The teacher questioned his pupils and they him. A student was expected to answer his teacher in the teacher's own words to ensure accuracy. The Jewish teachers were skillful in helping the student to memorize. Frank Graves notes the appeals made to the various types of memory—visual memory through reading, motor memory by oral recitation and writing, auditory memory by hearing, and musical memory by singing.[6] Mnemonic devices were also used. There were no vacations from this regimen except for Sabbaths and feast days. Discipline was used when necessary. Rewards in the forms of sweetmeats were common also.

After the age of 10 the Jewish boy entered the advanced training program. If his family was able to support him financially, he would study here until about the age of 15. The elementary school was called the Bethsepher or "house of the Midrash." Here the Midrash or oral law was studied. It became the custom that at age 13 a boy became a "son of the Law." At this point he became accountable before the Law as a man. Many boys ended their formal training about that time or shortly thereafter.

The Jewish teachers were well prepared for their task. *In addition to the synagogue schools there arose rabbinical schools for the training of teachers.* These usually came about spontaneously when some notable rabbi announced he would accept students. There was no fee involved. It was considered a religious duty to teach. Two rather notable rabbinical schools were established at Jerusalem by two great Pharisees, Hillel and Shammai. Saul of Tarsus studied in the school of Hillel under the great Gamaliel.

Those who entered the rabbinical schools did so at about age 15. The major method was still memorization. The chief content of the study was the Jewish commentaries. A major portion of the teaching consisted of the students questioning the teacher. Unlike our emphasis today, the success of a teacher's work was measured by the caliber of questions his pupils asked. By the time a Jewish boy was 18 he had learned a trade. Even the great rabbis had a trade by which they supported themselves. It was proverbial that a father who did not teach his son a trade taught him to steal.

In addition to his training, a teacher must be married since the mothers of the children might visit the school. No more than 25 pupils were to be put in charge of one teacher unless he had an assistant. If there were 50 pupils, another class was started. Everything was centered around the Scripture. For example, arithmetic was studied to enable the student to calculate the holy days and festivals and to compute his tithe.

In some ways, the Jews of intertestamental times did the best job with religious instruction that had ever been done in Israel. The Law received greater emphasis by the people as a whole than at any time since Moses. Many Jews could quote the entire Old Testament without error, and some could do the same with the oral law or tradition. Josephus boasted that the Jewish people knew the Law as well as their own names because the custom of beginning to study the Law at such an early age made an indelible impression.[7] Unfortunately, there was the tendency, just as there is on the part of some today, to become bogged down in theological hair-splitting which resulted in emphasis on details of the letter of the Law while ignoring the spirit. Ironically, the Jewish generation that rejected Christ was one of the most knowledgeable generations in antiquity as far as the Law of Moses was concerned.

From a positive viewpoint, the educational system of the post-exilic period was rather successful. First, it provided a means of instructing the Jewish youths wherever they were found. Jewish culture and history were passed to each succeeding generation through the combined efforts of home, synagogue, school, and temple observances. A result was a sense of patriotism and national pride. Emphasis on obedience to the Law was unfortunately marred by neglect of the deeper truths of the Law.

Summary

Religious education among the Jews must always be seen first as the work of God educating His people. In the Old Testament period, God worked through various agencies. In the earliest period of human history, He personally instructed men. The family has always been the keystone of education in every age. From time to time, God selected key individuals through which to work. He called Abraham to be the father of a nation. As such, Abraham had a vital role as a religious educator as did the patriarchs who followed him. With the exodus of Israel from Egypt and the giving of the Law, the congregation was assigned responsibility for education through parents, priests, and ritual. The faithful king also fostered education among his people. When parents, priests, and kings alike went astray, God raised up prophets to teach the nation God's ways. The Assyrian-Babylonian captivities were designed to teach Israel the folly of sin and the wisdom of obeying God's Word. It was only after the exile that the Jews founded the synagogue and formal schools for the teaching of their youth. These major ways of teaching the Jewish people are depicted in the following diagram:

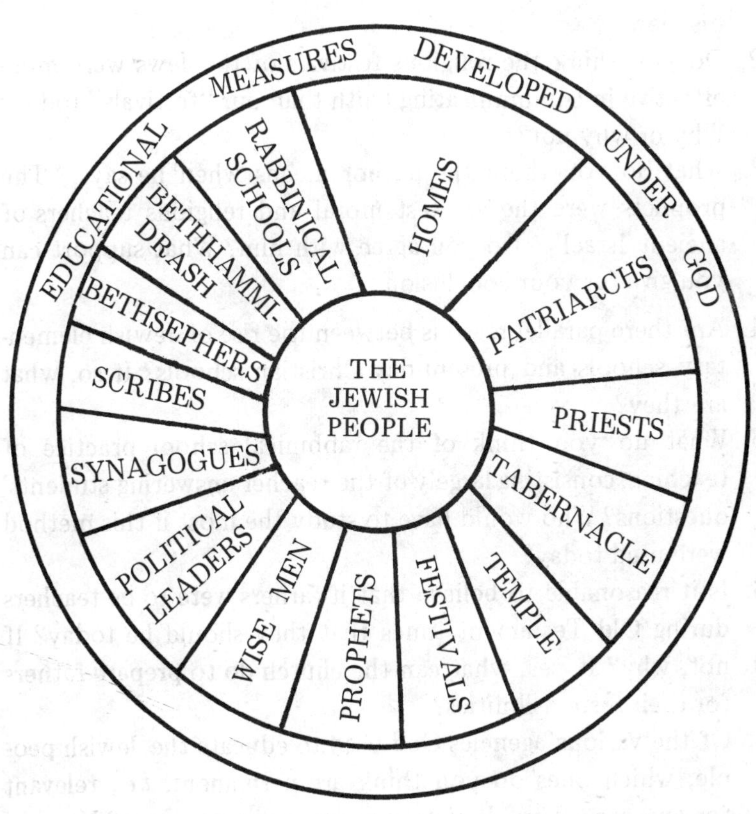
MEASURES
DEVELOPED
EDUCATIONAL
UNDER
RABBINICAL SCHOOLS
BETHHAMMI- DRASH
HOMES
GOD
BETHSEPHERS
PATRIARCHS
SCRIBES
THE JEWISH PEOPLE
PRIESTS
SYNAGOGUES
TABERNACLE
POLITICAL LEADERS
WISE MEN
PROPHETS
FESTIVALS
TEMPLE

Discussion Questions

1. Why might the author disagree with the statement that "drama has no place" in Christian education? Do you share his view?
2. Do you think the religious festivals of the Jews were more effective in communicating truth than our "festivals" today? Why or why not?
3. What do you think the author means when he says, "The prophets were the greatest moral and religious teachers of ancient Israel"? Do you agree with him? What support can you give for your conclusion?
4. Are there parallel reasons between the rise of Jewish elementary schools and present-day Christian schools? If so, what are they?
5. What do you think of the rabbinical school practice of teaching, consisting largely of the teacher answering students' questions? Who would have to study the most if this method were used today?
6. Is it reasonable to believe that if fathers were to be teachers during Old Testament times that they should be today? If not, why? If yes, what can the church do to prepare fathers for their responsibilities?
7. Of the various agencies God used to educate the Jewish people, which ones do you think are permanent, *i.e.*, relevant for any age? Why? Which ones are not permanent? How do you know?

Chapter III

New Testament Educational Practices

by Melvin L. Worthington

Introduction

The emphasis of much of the Old Testament is on different agencies that were used by the Jewish people to pass on God's revelation. In the New Testament, we discover a different emphasis. The gospels portray the pedagogical orientation of our Lord, and the epistles convey educational insights relevant to church education. Both sections of the New Testament illuminate early Christian educational practice or what we might call a philosophy of education.

Our philosophy of education indicates where we intend to take a student and what we plan to teach him. The New Testament philosophy of education is centered in God and concerned with mankind's learning how to live for the glory of God. This goal of Christian education influences the entire teaching-learning process. More specifically, this goal is reflected directly or indirectly as we comment on the following points: 1) educational purposes in the New Testament, 2) educational concepts in the New Testament, 3) educational methods in the New Testament, 4) educational principles in the New Testament, 5) educational individualization in the New Testament, and 6) educational standards in the New Testament. During the course of our study, we will use the words *training, education,* and *teaching* in a general sense. In reality, it is impossible to teach without training, to educate without teaching, or to train without teaching.

Educational Purposes in the New Testament

Great emphasis is given in the New Testament to the task of education. The scribes, Pharisees, and rabbis were in charge of Jewish education during the time of Christ. Most of the instruction was given in the home, although some of the young were trained in the synagogues.

The New Testament makes it clear that Jesus was a teacher first. He was a preacher, but a teacher primarily in the eyes of His contemporaries. During His ministry He taught with great influence and popularity. As He gathered around Him a group of learners or disciples, He taught them using many of the methods of the rabbis. *The purpose of His teaching was to perpetuate, through His followers, His own influence and work.* His teaching was with great authority and power. In the temple courts, synagogues, in private and in public places He taught.

Thus while we may think of Jesus as a preacher and healer, He was preeminently a teacher. Such terms as *Master, Rabbi,* and *Teacher* all point to the fact that the prominent function of His active ministry was teaching. The force of the Great Commission is teaching (Matthew 28:19-20). And in His last command the Lord emphasizes the task of teaching.

The task of teaching involves feeding the believer and directing his growth so that he may become what he can and should be. Eavey is correct, therefore, in saying that *the ultimate purpose of teaching is to bring the pupil into the likeness of God.* In terms of Christian teaching, effective teaching sets the conditions for the operation of divine grace in the heart and life of the pupil, thus transforming him into a man of God who is perfect, thoroughly furnished unto all good works.[1]

We see, then, that the task of the teacher is not some abstract idea that is unrelated to actual reality; for, there is no learning where there is no teaching. Rightly understood, learning and teaching are two aspects of the same process. In a good situation, both the teacher and the pupil learn when something is taught. Good teaching leads to better learning, and better learning should lead to better teaching. On this point, Eavey states that teaching is a means for controlling experiences so that learning will be in harmony with a predetermined purpose.[2] In order to have effective teaching, the environment must be organized for effective learning. No teacher has taught until there has been learning; and when there is not effective learning, effective teaching has not taken place. The uniqueness of the task of teaching is that the teacher organizes the environment and sets the stage for learning on the part of the pupil.

The effective teacher is like a craftsman using a variety of procedures, adapting methods to the particular pupils taught and objectives sought. Effective teaching is teaching adapted to individual needs, abilities, and personal characteristics of pupils. The uniqueness of our task is that it deals with the individual pupil as we seek to help, guide, and encourage a particular human being.[3]

The urgency of this hour is to develop men of God capable of undertaking the task of training and the purposes of the church. Without a strong and Scriptural educational program, it is impossible for us to effectively carry out the Great

Commission or to carry on the work of the church with a world-wide emphasis. Lack of training will always bring a warped view of training. No matter how gifted a person is, that person needs to develop his gifts through training. The church has the responsibility of training its workers and developing them into effective workers. Consequently, training is where our priority should be. No degree of Christian character and consistency will be maintained without a solid teaching and training program.

The purpose of Christian education and its urgency was well understood by the church in the apostolic age. Although the Apostles preached the gospel, they spent a great deal of time expounding the Scriptures. Such passages as Acts 2:42, 5:42, and 15:35 indicate that they spend much time in teaching.

One of the qualifications of the pastor today, just as in the apostolic period, is that he be a teacher. This is to be his primary function in the church. A pastor is to hold the truth, study the truth, teach the truth, apply the truth, and live the truth; and he is to be fully equipped to minister the truth (Titus 1:9; 1 Timothy 3:2, 4:13, 15; 2 Timothy 2:2).

The apostolic church enjoyed various spiritual gifts that enabled believers to be effective Christian educators (1 Corinthians 12:28; Ephesians 4:11). The work of the apostles as itinerant leaders and missionaries was largely that of teaching. Paul was called a teacher as well as an apostle. The prophets were men with special messages while the evangelists were itinerant preachers (Acts 8:40, 21:10-11). Individual churches were ministered to by permanent pastors who were also called bishops. Both laymen and those ordained were official teachers in the early church. The work of these official church teachers was regarded with the highest honor by the early church. They, like the pastors, resided permanently in local communities in contrast to apostles and evangelists who were considered itinerant church officers. James identifies himself with this class (James 1:1). As the first century drew to a close the Christian educational work of the church had been organized into a more systematic form, out of which there developed gradually the catechumenate of the early post-apostolic period.[4]

From a study of the Biblical record, we note that the entire evangelistic and missionary work of the apostolic church was educational in character. A certain amount of systematic Christian instruction was included in the work of the apostles, evangelists, pastors, and official church teachers throughout the early days of church history. One of the shortcomings of the church today is that it has substituted many things for teaching. Teaching is considered dull and boring and thus many show contempt and ridicule for the ministry of teaching. Without instruction, however, the Christian never will effectively witness for Christ nor will the church be the force in society it could be. It is time the church understood its purposes and undertook them: perpetuating the influence of Christ and leading pupils into the likeness of Christ.

Educational Concepts in the New Testament

A look at the educational terms used in the New Testament throws a great deal of light on teaching in Bible terms. The light manifested in these terms is profitable for our own times.

The Greek word *didasko*, "to teach" or "to instruct," means to either hold a discourse with others in order to instruct them or to speak to them where there may not be a direct personal and verbal participation. When we use it in the sense of instructing pupils, it describes the interlocutory method, which is the interplay of ideas and words between pupils and teachers. This is often called the discussion method today. When it is used in a didactic discourse where there are no direct interpersonal communications, it refers to the more formal monologues designed to give information (Matthew 4:23; 5-7; 13:36). A teacher, then, is an instructor and should have the ability and fitness for the task.

Another term that appears in the New Testament is *manthano*, "to learn," which stresses the main point of teaching: to cause a person to learn. Teaching and learning are dynamic and imply personal activity and interaction (Matthew 11:29; 28:19).

The Greek word *paratithemi*, "to place beside," is related to the English word *presentation*. Indicated by this word is the thought of presenting an idea which is essential in the teaching process, and it is associated with the principle of adaptation. This is seen in Christ's use of parables in His teaching. In using parables Christ employed the figure of placing alongside of, or near one, hence before Him in an accessible position. Teaching should be sound and adapted to the capacity and development of the recipient (Matthew 13:24; Mark 8:6).

Elucidate is a term that is comparable to the Greek word *diermeneuo*. Elucidation or interpretation sets forth the responsiblity of the teacher to make clear the truth and to effectively edify a hearer. Christ sets this example in Luke 24:27. Other illustrations of this practice are found in 1 Corinthians 12:30, 14:5, 13, 27.

In addition to Greek words that convey the ideas of

instruction, acquisition, presentation, and elucidation, we also find a Greek word, *ektithemi*, that signifies the bringing out of the latent and hidden ideas of a passage or a system of thought and life. Educational exposition is true teaching (Acts 11:4; 18:26; 28:23).

Before examining the methods illustrated in the New Testament, let us briefly look at three additional New Testament terms: *prophetes*, *poimen*, and *episkopos*. The first of these words, *prophetes*, "one who speaks," sets forth the idea that God gave a message to a man and he spoke that message to people. Such things as their failures, achievements, privileges, glory, responsibilities, and future doom might be treated. The message and authority of the prophet came from God (Deuteronomy 18:15-22). Old Testament teachers, Jesus, John the Baptist, and special speakers in the apostolic age were referred to by this word (Matthew 5:12; Acts 3:25; 1 Corinthians 14:29, 37).

The next word, *poimen*, "a shepherd," suggests one who tends a flock. By analogy it refers to a person who gives mental and spiritual nourishment while guarding and supporting those under his care (John 10:2, 16; 1 Peter 2:25). In exercising this care, the chief prerequisite is love (John 21:15-18). In carrying out this duty, great diligence and humility must be evident as the divine gifts and appointments of the Holy Spirit are recognized (Acts 20:28).

The word *overseer*, coming from the Greek *episkopos*, signifies that the bishop is to feed and protect the flock (Acts 20:28). As we have noted earlier, one of the qualifications of a bishop is that he have the aptitude to teach (1 Timothy 3:2; Titus 1:9). Christ is referred to as the Chief Shepherd and Bishop (1 Peter 2:25).[5]

Educational Methods in the New Testament

The teaching methods of the scribes and rabbis were not much different from the practice of those of earlier centuries. Their main objective seemed to be memorization or the exact reproduction of the master's teaching by the pupil. During New Testament times the voice of prophecy had become silent and the canon of revealed truth was considered complete; thus the only aim was the intellectual mastery and interpretation of this sacred revelation. In practice the religious leaders sought to develop strict habits of ritualistic observance of the precepts of the law as a condition for association and fellowship with the selected company of true Israelites, *e.g.*, the scribes and the Pharisees. The scribes and Pharisees sought to utilize every method and means to secure and hold the attention of their pupils in order to make their memories the trained and obedient servants of an educational ideal. It should be noted that their orientation was a very narrow one (Matthew 23).

In spite of the fact that the defects in their system caused them not to be able to separate clearly the gold from the dross in their inherited teachings, or to adapt to the urgent needs of the common people, five valuable results were achieved through their teachings: a) it developed a test for close, critical study; b) it sharpened the wits, even to the point of perversity; c) it formed a powerful bond of union among the Jewish people; d) it encouraged a reverence for law and produced desirable social conduct; e) it prepared the way for the Christian view of God.

The claim that Jesus was a master teacher has already been examined and is borne out by every inquiry, test, and comparison that modern educational science can apply to His work and influence. Jesus in both His message and method injects a new note of authority which challenged attention and inspired confidence. The life philosophy of Jesus made His teachings imperishable. He reached out to men with a keen insight into life and drew them to Him. With simple directness of speech, He addressed the consciences and wills of men as He set forth the ideal of the higher life and as He sought to lift them to the plane of fellowship with Himself in thought and action.[6]

Christ accomplished His goals because He appealed to the needs of those who listened to Him. On the subject of needs, Eavey suggests a sixfold classification: a) basic physiological needs (sex, sleep, rest); b) love needs (companionship, sense of belonging, affection); c) recognition (self-respect, being accepted and appreciated by others); d) adventure and experimentation (excitement, stimulation, movement); e) self-realization (liberty to achieve and to develop in one's own way); f) religious or spiritual needs (need for communion, worship, fellowship with a higher power. The satisfying of these needs is the process of learning.[7]

Educational Principles in the New Testament

Purpose for learning emerges when adjustments are made by an individual in order to meet his or her basic needs. Christ knew, therefore, that effective techniques of teaching and training must take into account the basic needs of the students. To be effective teachers requires that we not only learn procedures, techniques and methods, but that we understand principles which are basic. Concentrating on methods and procedures will tend to cause us to violate principles, and this will result in ineffective teaching and learning. When we focus on the right principles of learning and teaching, the choice of methods and procedures can be made intelligently. In choosing and using methods and procedures for effective teaching, the criteria must always be the principles of teaching. To be effective teachers, therefore, we must adhere to basic principles in organizing and guiding learning.

Since methods and procedures must be based on the principles of the learning process, we must determine the principles of learning in the Scriptures. In the light of the principles of learning, we will be better able to understand that the methods and procedures of the Lord Jesus and the Apostles were mere aids to help the learning process. One principle of learning is that the presentation of information is vital to the learning process. Among other passages, Matthew 5-7 and John 13-17 are passages that establish this basic principle. Various methods of giving information are illustrated in each passage. Parables, lectures, illustrations, questions, and discussions are just a few methods utilized.

Another principle is that information is made practical and understandable by the use of illustrations. By parables, allegories, visual aids, and miracles, the New Testament writers sought to make their material practical. For instance, Jesus used the Old Testament Scriptures to illustrate His teaching and so did the writer of Hebrews. Parables are earthly stories to illustrate eternal truth. A key to successful education is the proper use of illustrations. The illustration serves as a window for the material to shine into the heart and mind of the learner. Such passages as Matthew 5 and Hebrews 11 establish this principle of learning.

An additional principle is that the student learns by doing or by experience. The Biblical writers in the New Testament utilized this principle of learning in their writings. Truth, for it to be learned, must be practiced. Participation is vital to the process of learning. Such passages as Matthew 10 and John 15 establish this principle.

Some have chosen to call a fourth principle the principle of motivation or inspiration. No matter what name we apply to it, we must be aware that inspiration is a principle in the learning process. The pupil must be challenged to achieve and to fulfill his or her aspirations. Romans 16 and 2 Timothy 4 are passages that establish this principle of learning. Many methods might be used to inspire or motivate in the learning process. The methods must be adapted to the individual, but based on this vital principle of learning.

The curiosity of the pupil has a great deal to do with the learning process. In selecting methods and procedures, we must keep in mind that inquiry and interest are basics in the learning process. The methods we select serve as aids to heighten and stimulate the curiosity of the pupil. Such passages as John 3 and Matthew 13 establish this fifth principle of learning. A careful study of these passages will make one conscious of the importance of inquisitiveness in learning.

The principle of incentive must also be taken into consideration. Giving rewards and awards are methods and procedures based on the principle of incentive. When we recognize that this is a principle of learning, it will enable us to utilize many methods that will aid the learning process. Matthew 24, Philippians 3, and 1 Thessalonians 4 illustrate this principle. It should be noted that in the addresses to the Asian assemblies in Revelation 2-3, this principle is repeatedly used.

A key principle in the process of learning which is often overlooked is that of looking inward to see how we really are on the inside. Effective methods of teaching must keep this principle in mind and utilize it to cause the student to take an inward look. Matthew 23, 2 Corinthians 13:5-7, and Philippians 4:6-9 clearly establish this principle of learning. Subjective evaluation is vital to the learning process.

When the teacher uses the method of question and answer he is acknowledging consciously or unconsciously that interrogation is a vital principle in the learning process. Many times methods are used and people do not understand why they are to be used or why they work. Methods based on the principles of learning will always work if they are adapted to the individual situation. This principle is seen in Matthew 22 and John 20.

A ninth principle of learning is set forth by Paul in 2 Timothy 3 and Philippians 3. Paul charged those in Corinth to be imitators of him as he was of Christ (11:1) and those in Ephesus to be imitators of God (Ephesians 5:1). One of the great principles of learning is that we imitate what we see. The teacher teaches by example and others follow that example. The key to effective teaching is not only the method or procedure used, but the teacher. The teacher must be an example of the message he teaches. The effectiveness of the teaching of Jesus was due to the fact that His life exemplified the truths He taught.

As a tenth principle of learning, we will briefly look at an idea mentioned by Luke (Acts 17:10-15) and by John (John 5:39-47). We need to challenge our students to investigate and learn for themselves. Methods and techniques of teaching must be utilized in the light of this principle of learning. Students must be stimulated to search out for themselves truth and then to come to their own conclusions. This principle of investigation is essential to developing mature, zealous Christians.

In the light of this principle, perhaps we should search individually the Scriptures for further principles of learning. Before considering this suggestion, however, let us just list what may be additional Biblical principles of learning. Among these principles we find the ensuing: 1) the principle of illumination (1 Corinthians 2:14), 2) the principle of intercession (Acts 4, 12, 27), and 3) the principle of integration (John 3, 4).

Educational Individualization in the New Testament

As we have previously stressed, an effective teacher must realize that methods and procedures are developed in the light of the principles of learning. The learning process is basically the same, but our methods and procedures must be adapted to those individuals to whom we are ministering. In other words, our methods will need to be flexible to meet the needs of particular pupils. As the perfect teacher, Jesus used appropriate methods, for He understood His pupils perfectly. He knew what was in people and taught truth so they were able to understand it (John 2:24, 25; Mark 4:33). It is interesting to note that many things He wanted to teach His pupils they were not ready for and thus He refrained from teaching them (John 16:12; Luke 24:27). A study of the teaching methods of Christ will reveal that He used different methods and procedures in dealing with different individuals. Effective techniques will be utilized to minister to individual pupils whether there is one individual or a group.

When we analyze the methods of Christ, we note first His approach. Nearly half of the teaching in the ministry of Jesus was initiated by the learners themselves. The other half was initiated by Christ. He usually started on a personal level. Next we notice there is nothing stereotyped about His pattern; for in each case the learner and his need were different. Christ started where the pupil was and let the pupil's readiness and response guide the learning process. Many times what Jesus did was determined by what His pupils did. Christ encouraged questions and used them to enable His learners to learn. He relied a great deal on deeds which gave Him an opportunity to speak to those who had observed the deeds. The Gospels reveal a steady progress of content and experience climaxing in who Jesus was and what He came to do. Finally, we observe the mixed reactions that accompanied the teaching of Christ. Some marveled in unbelief; some responded by believing; and others simply ignored His teaching (Matthew 7:28, 29; Luke 15:1, 2; Matthew 8:34).[9]

Educational Standards in the New Testament

Our definition of training is that it is a process whereby one person takes another from where he is to where he ought to be. A standard is before us and we seek to carry our pupils toward that standard. The Pharisees sought to get their pupils to meet certain external standards (Matthew 23). They were primarily interested in getting their followers to conform to certain external practices. Christ's teaching dealt with the internal. He sought to get His followers not merely to conform to certain external practices, but to have an internal change that would manifest itself in external practices. One of the fundamental differences, then, between the teachings of the Pharisees and of Christ was that they went from the outside in whereas

Christ went from the inside out. Christ knew that a man could be externally obedient and not have a changed heart, but it was impossible to have an internal change and it not be manifested on the outside. A study of Matthew 23 clearly establishes, then, that the first standard of Christian education is the internalization of truth in such a manner that a person outwardly reflects the truth believed.

We must not, nevertheless, overlook the fact that learning is a process. As babes we are to develop and grow to maturity. Knowledge in itself is sterile or useless. Learning has to do with the way we act or behave, and God made man to learn. Learning involves, then, a change in behavior. Furthermore, learning is a dynamic process that cannot be touched directly by human beings but can be controlled in part. This process goes on continually. We can control the conditions but not the process. Thus, growing in Christ is the second standard of being trained in New Testament truths. Actually, there is perhaps only one overall standard for Christian education; that is, whether people are outwardly reflecting the inwardly believed truths of God. That is to say, people are being transformed from babes in Christ to mature disciples of Christ.

Conclusion

The basic principles of education are found in the Scriptures. The Scriptures, therefore, are our rule for teaching and learning just as they are for doctrine and behavior. We must not only get our content from the Scriptures but our principles of teaching also. In turn, *Biblical learning must determine our methods of teaching.* When this is forgotten, our teaching will be ineffective and the learning process will be hindered. It is impossible to teach the right material with the wrong method. Let us be thoroughly Scriptural in our understanding of education and be sure that our purposes, methods, principles, and standards are adapted to each follower of Christ. If we do this, we will be practicing the philosophy of education implied in the New Testament.

Discussion Questions

1. Do you agree with the author's statement that the pastor's "primary function in the church" is to be a teacher? Why?
2. What, according to the author, is the difference between a method of teaching and a principle of teaching? Is he correct? Defend your position.
3. Why does the author argue that the methods of education must be based upon the principles of education? Evaluate his viewpoint.
4. What problems, if any, are involved in getting students "to search out for themselves truth and then to come to their own conclusions"? Is the goal worth the problems involved?
5. The author says, "It is interesting to note that many things He (Christ) wanted to teach His pupils they were not ready for and thus He refrained from teaching them." What was it about Christ's pupils that made them ill-prepared for His messages?
6. How does the author define training? Do you accept this definition? Why or why not?
7. If we should stress internalizing the teachings of Christ, is it ever appropriate to demand a mere external obedience to

them? If it is appropriate, why and when? If always inappropriate, why?

8. Is it not dangerous to simply stress the internalization of Christian truth as well as it is to merely emphasize external conformity to Christian standards? If it is dangerous, how can we avoid both dangers?

Chapter IV

The Major Objectives Of The Church

by Robert E. Picirilli

Introduction

We do not encounter much controversy about the major objectives of the church when we speak of them as getting people to learn how "to live for the glory of God" and "to bring the pupil into the likeness of God" as we have done in our last chapter. Controversy arises when we hear some earnest advocate of missions or evangelism say that the primary task of the church is *evangelism*, to win the lost or evangelize the world. Or, it arises when a brother with a different emphasis responds: Our objective is *edification*, the building up of believers, the strengthening of the saints. And the church gets torn by a tragic and divisive debate about its chief goal. Each side, equally sincere and armed with enough Scripture texts for overkill, firmly believes that the other side must be persuaded to get its priorities right, to recognize what our number one work is, to work for what is "nearest and dearest to the heart of God."

The Scriptural Goal of the Church

Must we decide which is primary, evangelism or edification? Do we have to identify with these or those, who advocate one or the other? Or can these apparently antagonistic positions be reconciled? And if there is a convincing answer to such questions, where will we find it? By comparing the numbers attending churches with various emphases? Or by examining budgets of the most prosperous churches? No. If there is an answer for us who believe that the Bible is the very perfect Word of God, we will find the answer there. Whatever the Scriptures say—that will have to guide us.

Then let us search the Scriptures: first, the most famous passage of all, the Great Commission of Matthew 28:18-20:

> Jesus said to them: "All authority in heaven and upon earth was given to me. Therefore, going, make disciples of all the nations, baptizing them in the name of the Father and the Son and the Holy Spirit, teaching them to be keeping all things that I ever commanded you. And behold I am with you all the days until the end of the age."[1]

The weight of these words is obvious. This was the essence of what Jesus discussed with His disciples during the forty days after His resurrection when He was "being seen of them . . . and speaking of the things pertaining to the kingdom of God" (Acts 1:3). In one set of words or another, this Commission finds its way into every one of the four gospels and Acts. We do not expect to find, here, a detailed explanation of all the church's work; still, this Great Commission, like a stethoscope on a beating heart, focuses our attention on the pulsing drive of the church's task.

There is just one imperative verb in this Commission. Focus first on that command: make disciples. The word *disciple* comes from the word for learning. (Our word *mathematics*, as a structured and formalized kind of learning, comes from the same word.) A disciple is a learner, in a deliberate and formal sense, one who submits to the discipline of instruction and training, a student, an apprentice, a pupil, a follower.

Connected with that one command are three equal participles, each one essential to the main imperative, each one indicating an important part of the work of making disciples. The first is *going*. The church has to be on the move to do its work, and the *"all the nations"* attached to the command defines precisely the arena in which the going must take place.

The second participle is *baptizing*. Since baptism is meant to be a person's public profession of faith in Jesus Christ, this participle marks the conversion of those who obey the gospel preached as we go. They "turned to God from idols" (1 Thessalonians 1:9). They confess that the old man was "buried with him by baptism into death," and that a new man arose from those waters to "walk in newness of life" (Romans 6:1-11).

The third participle is *teaching*. A disciple is more than a convert; he is a learner, a pupil. Then there must be formal instruction. And Jesus said that everything He had ever commanded must be taught to those baptized. Furthermore, they must be taught to be keeping all these things—a continuing action that means a habitual and practiced way of life. Diagram it this way:

<table>
<tr><td>Make disciples, by</td><td>going
baptizing
teaching.</td></tr>
</table>

The three are all part of the one: going with the gospel (cf. Mark 16:15), baptizing those who believe (cf. Mark 16:16a), and instructing those who are baptized in all the ways of living in submission to the teachings of Christ. Why must we choose one of these against the other, or give one priority? No reason at all: all three are equally essential to the task.

We turn to another passage, one which shows us just how that premier missionary Paul conceived of his task. He was but one man, of course, with his own particular gifts and thus his own individual threads to weave into the pattern of the whole cloth. No one man can expect to accomplish the objectives of the whole church. But every one can keep that ultimate goal in his eye and present his own work in those terms.

Colossians 1:20-29 shows us how Paul understood his own work as "a minister"—a servant—both of the gospel (verse 23) and of the church (verse 25). We examine the climactic part of this passage, especially, verses 28, 29:

> We proclaim Christ, admonishing each person and teaching each person, with the utmost wisdom, in order that we may present each person complete in Christ; for which purpose, yea, I labor, striving according to His in-working which is being in-worked in me powerfully.[2]

The key part of this is the ultimate purpose of Paul's labor. That purpose is: "in order that we may present each person complete (mature, perfect) in Christ." We will appreciate this more, in its context, if we look back earlier in the chapter. In verses 20-22, Paul summarized the work of Christ as the work of reconciliation by His death on the cross. Note verse 22, in particular, where the ultimate objective of Christ's atoning death is: "to present you holy and unblameable and unreproveable" before God.

In other words, Christ died to reconcile men so that, in the end, He could present holy, unblameable (unblemished), unreproveable (irreproachable) persons to God. And when Paul moves on, from the end of verse 23, to describe his own personal work as a minister of the gospel, he contemplates the same ultimate objective. Note the same verb, *"present,"* in verses 22 and 28; and the "complete (perfect) person" of verse 28 is precisely the "holy and unblameable and unreproveable" person in verse 22. Whatever the objective of Christ's work, that is the objective of Paul's work.

Paul's final purpose, then, was to offer up to God, when Jesus returns, persons brought to maturity in Christ, holy and without blemish and irreproachable (cf. 1 Thessalonians 2:19 and 3:13). To this end he labored; for this purpose he proclaimed the Christ who also died for that very same objective.

And what did this proclaiming of Christ include? Evangelization, certainly, for the proclamation of Christ, by whose death God "hath reconciled us to himself" (2 Corinthians 5:18) begins with "we pray you in Christ's stead, be ye reconciled to God" (2 Corinthians 5:20). But, as in the Great Commission, mere conversion is not all. In Colossians 1:28 the main verb—we proclaim Christ—is explained by two participles this time: admonishing and teaching. Both of these (certainly the latter) deal with Paul's ministry to the ones converted. Their correction and teaching was just as much part of proclaiming Christ as their evangelization. Building them up in the faith was just as essential to the ultimate objective of presenting perfect saints to

God as converting them.

Paul would have been silly to think about presenting mature saints to God, as the fruit of his ministry, if he had ignored evangelism. He would have had none to offer. He would have been equally silly to think about presenting mature saints to God if he had neglected their spiritual progress after their conversion. He would have had babes in Christ, at best, to offer. We had better not neglect the edification that brings believers from "babes in Christ" (1 Corinthians 3:1) to "complete in Christ" (Colossians 1:28), for in that maturing is to be found the stability on which their final presentation to God is predicated (Colossians 1:22, 23).

Once again, why must we choose between evangelism and edification? We need not. Both are equally essential in the proclamation of Christ that aims at achieving the objective of His own work, the presentation of holy, blameless, irreproveable persons to God.

One more passage merits close examination. There we find, not Christ's Commission to the disciples, or Paul's concept of his own ministry, but a picture of the organic functioning of the church. That picture is in Ephesians 4:11-16. Here are the two most critical verses, 11 and 12:

> He (Christ) gave, as one group, the apostles; as another, the prophets; for another, the evangelizers; and for another, the shepherds and teachers—with a view to the equipping of the saints for a work of service, for building the body of Christ.3

These two verses give an introductory summary of a picture that might be entitled, the functioning of the church toward its objective. Then verses 13-16 develop that picture in explanatory detail. Some of the aspects of this picture are well worth our closer examination.

Note, first, that the objective toward which the church functions is found in the words, "for building the body of Christ," as given in verse 12. Essentially the same words are repeated at the end of verse 16: "the whole body . . . maketh increase of the body unto the edifying of itself in love."

The edifying (building) of the body includes two things. The first of these is the enlargement that comes by evangelism. While this aspect of the building up of the body of Christ is not so prominent in Ephesians, "edify" implies it. To edify is, literally, to build, as when erecting a building; and necessary to the erection of a building is the bringing in of the building materials. For a stone building, for example, new stones must be cut from the quarry and brought to the building site. In Ephesians 2:19-22 (and in 1 Peter 2:5) individual believers are regarded as living stones being built into a holy temple for the Lord's habitation. Therefore, the "increase of the body" in Ephesians 4:16 may well include enlargement by winning converts to Christ.

The other thing included in the "building of the body of Christ" is the strengthening and establishing of those won—their spiritual growth, in other words. If stones must be cut and brought to the building site, they must also be polished and fitted into the building. The passage before us says a great deal about the believer's growth. In verse 13, the ideal of a "perfect" (*i.e.*, mature, complete) person is upheld. And the standard by which that ideal is measured is the full stature of Christ Himself. Verse 14 continues this line by showing the weakness of persons who remain spiritual children (Greek: babes) and are as unstable as small craft in a wind storm, subject to cunning, deceptive doctrine. The solution to this spiritual immaturity is presented in verse 15, in the injuction to "grow up." The word is the normal one for growth, as in growth of a plant. It is the same as the word *increase* in verse 16. Every verse, then, from 12 to 16, says something about spiritual growth as an essential part of the building up of the body of Christ.

Here in Ephesians 4:11, 12 are several phrases about purpose, all built on the giving of spiritual gifts cited in verse 11. The first phrase is "with a view to the equipping of the saints" (AV, "for the perfecting of the saints"). Since verse 11 mentions only the leadership gifts, the point is that these leaders are given to the church, first of all, to equip, perfect the saints. That "equipping" includes (1) everything that needs to be done to foster the spiritual growth and stability of the saints, and (2) everything that needs to be done to help the saints find their own places of service and develop the abilities needed to function in those places.

The second purpose phrase is: "for a work of service" (AV, "for the work of the ministry"). The comma that separates this phrase from the previous one can easily mislead the reader. Clearly, this phrase builds on the previous one and means that all the saints are being equipped for a work of service. Every believer has a ministry to perform in the functioning of the church toward its objective.

The third purpose phrase is: "for building the body of Christ" (AV, "for the edifying of the body of Christ"). And this phrase builds on the previous one, thus identifying the ultimate objective of the service for which the saints are being equipped. We have already examined, above, the two-fold meaning of this building of the body by enlargement and establishment.

Read these verses this way, then:
1) the apostles, prophets, evangelists, and pastor-teachers
2) equip the saints (including themselves),
3) and the equipped saints perform service
4) aimed at the building of the church by evangelism and
   edification.

Verse 16 presents this same picture in a very interesting way, using the human body as an illustration. Jesus is the head of the body (verse 15) and from Him issues the functioning of the whole body toward its objective of "making increase of the body unto the edifying (building) of itself in love." The nature of that functioning is likened to the way the various parts of the human body work together. The words "fitly joined together" and "compacted" and "that which every joint supplieth" give us an uncomplicated picture of the way the human body, with all its various parts, is jointed and nourished together for a harmonious functioning (cf. Colossians 2:19). All the muscles and ligaments and joints and bones bind together the various parts, and all these receive their (neurological) impulses from the head, and all this produces a smoothly functioning whole.

In exactly the same way, all the members of Christ's body have their own distinct functions (compare 1 Corinthians 12:12-27). Like the eyes, feet, ears, and hands, and like the muscles, sinews, ligaments, joints, and vessels of the human body, all believers are "impulsed" from the Head ("the effectual working, energizing, in the measure of every part") and under His direction are being enabled to function together, in their infinite and purposeful variety, as a beautifully harmonious unity. And all of this toward the building—by enlargement and establishment—of that body, the Church.

Once more, then, must we choose between evangelism and

edification? Certainly not. Here in Ephesians we have been given a picture of the ultimate objective of the church as the building of the body of Christ, with all believers playing various parts in the service that aims at that building. And that building up needs enlargement by evangelistic outreach (note the evangelists in verse 11) as much as it needs the establishment and maturity of those won (note the pastors-teachers in verse 11). We have seen the same kind of picture in Colossians 1:20-29 where Paul's own concept of his ministry is described. And we have seen the same kind of picture in the Great Commission.

If we are to fulfill the Great Commission and make disciples; if we are to conceive of our work as Paul did his own, as an extension of the work of Christ, aimed at presenting mature persons to God; if we are to function in our churches, like the Bible pictures the church as functioning, toward the building of Christ's body; in short, if we have a Biblical objective, we must avoid fragmenting the church by creating a tension between evangelism and edification. If sides have to be chosen, if some say that our primary task is evangelism and we only edify the saints to enable them to evangelize, or if others say that a church's purpose is to edify the saints and evangelism is subordinate to that—if any of these things happen, those who are responsible are guilty of sin. They have irresponsibly created division and neglected God's imperative.

The Two Major Tasks of the Church

In the foregoing, the overall objective of the church has been expressed in at least three different ways: the making of disciples, the presenting of mature persons to God, the building of the body of Christ. All these say the same thing. For our better understanding of this overall objective, though, we will do well to examine more closely the two major aims that are incorporated into it. The remainder of this chapter will be devoted to that examination.

Evangelism is primary, so long as we understand *primary* to mean that it comes first in the order of our attention, not that it is more important. Evangelism is primary simply because that is the method by which each individual is brought into the church. Whatever else the church has to do toward making a disciple of a person, that person must first be baptized in the name of the Father, Son, and Holy Spirit. That baptism—understood in its true sense as the act of public profession of conversion to Christ—is the aim and immediate fruit of evangelism.

The categorical imperative to evangelize is the business of the church and of every member of the church. One can hardly understand the New Testament without perceiving the nature and importance of the evangelistic thrust. In the first place, this responsibility to evangelize is at the heart of the compulsion of the church to go. The Great Commission assumes, as we saw earlier, a church going into all nations and making disciples there. It is of the very essence of the church to go.

In the second place, it is of the very essence of the gospel that all men ought to be evangelized. The very definition of the gospel is that it is "the power of God for salvation to *any* one who believes" (Romans 1:14-16). The very thing the gospel announces is: "*Whosoever* shall call on the name of the Lord shall be saved" (Romans 10:13). Paul says the gospel was being preached when God said to Abraham, "In thee shall *all* nations be blessed" (Galatians 3:8). In Colossians 1:6 Paul wrote that the gospel had come to his readers "as it is in *all* the world." In Colossians 1:23 he referred to the gospel as "preached to *every* creature which is under heaven." In Titus 2:11 he reported that "The grace of God that bringeth salvation hath appeared to *all* men." Whatever else these last three difficult references may mean, the very least they can mean is that the very essence of gospel proclamation is that it is proclaimed for *all*.

In the third place, it is of the very essence of a Christian to be a witness to the unconverted world. Much New Testament material could be gathered to make this point; perhaps two items will do here. In Matthew 5:1-16, Jesus described the citizens of God's Kingdom as poor in spirit, mourning, meek, hungry for righteousness, merciful, pure in heart. In these (spiritual) characteristics they manifest the character of their heavenly King and Father, and so are salt in the earth, light to the world. When men see this living witness, they will be caused to glorify God (compare 1 Peter 2:9-12). Thus, the very nature of a citizen of the Kingdom of God, in his sojourning on earth, is to be a witness to the unconverted, by life and lip, by his being and doing and saying.

Equally interesting and significant is the emphasis, in Acts, on the disciples as witnesses. This was obviously one of the themes Luke was conscious of. At the close of his gospel Luke recorded that the risen Jesus spoke to the disciples of His death and resurrection and said: "Ye are *witnesses* of these things" (Luke 24:48). That motif was taken up immediately in Acts, when Jesus commanded the tarrying and promised the anointing: "and ye shall be *witnesses* unto me" (Acts 1:8). The motif continues in 1:22, 2:32, 3:15, 4:33, and 5:32, each verse consciously using the word *witnesses* to describe the disciples.

The conclusion is irresistible: the very nature of being a

Christian is to be a witness to the unconverted world. That is at the heart of evangelism. Here is a question, though: does this mean the same thing as saying that all believers are soul winners? Yes and no. If one means, by soul winner, the successful converter of the unsaved, the one who actually prays with them in the act of decision, then we may as well face the truth that not all believers are—or necessarily should be—as successful soul winners as some. But if one means that every believer is aiming at the winning of souls by his witness, then every believer ought to be a soul winner.

In other words, every Christian ought to recognize that evangelistic outreach is a part of the very essence of the church's (and his) objective. And every Christian ought to be aware that his own unhindered witness to the unconverted is essential to that evangelistic outreach. And every Christian, regardless what particular part he may personally play in reaching toward that objective, ought to be developed to fill his role in the enlargement of the body as effectively as possible.

This certainly means that some believers will have greater effectiveness as evangelists than others. The Bible leaves us no doubt on this, for only to *some* is given the gift of being an evangelist (Ephesians 4:11). This does not mean that the rest are delivered from the responsibility of evangelizing, any more than the fact that some Christians have a special gift for showing mercy (Romans 12:8) delivers the rest from the responsibility to be merciful (cf. Matthew 5:7). All Christians should be evangelizing; some have a special gift for evangelizing. This understanding frees us from two errors. On the one hand, none can be free from the responsibility of evangelization. On the other hand, we expect some to have the specific work of evangelism as more their primary role than others.

Let me say one thing more about this responsibility of the church to build itself by enlargement through the evangelization of the unconverted. That responsibility is perverted when churchmen make comparative numbers the basis for their decisions about when and where to evangelize. We hear some say, these days, that one ought to invest his money only in that work where the largest number of souls per dollar will be won. Some use this standard to downgrade foreign missions, for example, mocking the efforts of a missionary who gathers a little group. Some use this standard to decide where to build a church: establish a church, they say, only in the population centers where the people are, and where one can soon get a thousand in Sunday school. Well, no doubt there are more people in a metropolis than in a small town or country community. And no doubt one can reach a thousand quicker in a city in the United States than in a jungle village (or even a city) in Africa or India. But the Lord's commission to evangelize knows no national or populational boundaries. The gospel is for all, at home or abroad, rural or urban. It is a wicked travesty of the Great Commission to use "dollars per soul" or "souls per hour of work invested" as the basis for decisions about when and where to evangelize.

Similarly misguided are appeals based on special interest groups. One voice tells us we ought to have a church in the inner cities. Another calls us to evangelize the Cubans in Miami, or the reservation Indians, or the blacks, or the "down and out," or even "the up and out." Well, no doubt all these need evangelization, but they do not *specially* need it. There are no special needs for evangelization in the Great Commission. The needs of the poor and wealthy and middle class, the black and white and red and swarthy, the "in crowd" and outcast, the

citizen and displaced are all the same. There is no difference—
not in their need or in our responsibility—for all have sinned.
The gospel is for all who have sinned. The most moving appeals
are those made when one servant of God says, "God wants *me*
there." The whole church is responsible for the whole world,
and in the providence of God, some are put here or there, at
this time or that, to fulfill their particular roles as witnesses.

Now let us turn our attention to edification. The edification of believers is quite as important as the evangelism of the
lost, an importance tragically blunted when some tip their hats
to edification by saying that the saints only need to be edified
so as to be able to win others. It is time we came to appreciate
the growth of the believer toward spiritual maturity as an end in
itself, and not merely as a means to an end.

This end is of great value to God, and in that value is
found the justification for our attention to the work of
edification. The Great Commission, as we saw, included not
only the responsibility to baptize converts, but also the
responsibility to teach, to educate the converts in the careful
observance of all the things taught by Jesus. Paul's concept of
the ultimate end of Jesus' work was to present holy and
unblemished and irreproachable believers to God (Colossians
1:22). Consequently, Paul saw the objective of his own labor as
to "present every man perfect (mature, complete) in Christ
Jesus" (Colossians 1:28). Clearly, then, the life of a believer
who observes all the principles set forth in the teachings of
Jesus is of worth to God. He delights in observing that child of
His who walks in His ways. The presentation of mature saints to
God at Christ's coming will be the occasion for great joy (1
Thessalonians 2:19, 20; 3:13). God will be glorified in the
perfection shown in such saints. The work of Christ will be

praised as having achieved its goal. The angels will delight in the beauty displayed in the saints' character, and will glorify God and Christ.

We had better not be like the poet who wrote: "Full many a gem of purest ray serene the dark unfathomed caves of ocean bear; full many a flower is born to blush unseen and waste its sweetness on the desert air." But the beauty of a flower is not wasted just because it cannot be *used:* worn on some lady's breast, displayed on some banquet table. The brilliant glow of some gem is not wasted if it is not *used:* polished and set, adorning golden ring or jeweled crown. There was never bud or bloom whose gentle fragrance was wasted, not if God saw and sniffed its sweet perfume; never ruby red or emerald green whose flashing colors were uselessly spent, not if God saw and delighted in the beauty He made.

Just so, a utilitarian philosophy often twists our concept of the Christian life. The flourishing, flowering, fruitful Christian life is a thing of beauty and worthwhile for that reason and for no other. Such a trophy of grace is the goal of God's saving work, and in such a life God exults. He is glad and glorified.

One more look at Ephesians 4:11-16 should prove helpful here. We already noted that much is said there about the importance of the maturing of the saints toward the final goal of the building of the body. Paul spoke of the tragedy of spiritual children (infants, babes) who are compared (verse 14) to small, unstable sailing craft caught in a storm, at the mercy of waves and wind, tossed helplessly this way and that. Far too many believers are like this, agitated and tossed, fickle and vacillating, following first one voice and then another, unstable before every shifting wind of false doctrine.

The solution is that believers "grow up into him in all

things" (verse 15), that each believer become "a perfect man" (verse 13). And how is that perfection, that maturity to be measured? When is the growth complete? Paul gives us a precise answer: "unto the measure of the stature of the fulness of Christ" (verse 13). In other words, the goal of spiritual growth is to bring the believer to the place where he measures up to the full stature of ideal humanity reached in Jesus Christ Himself. The end is nothing less than that. No wonder God will take delight in, and be glorified in, the presentation of mature saints to Himself at Christ's return.

We cannot consider this without going to Romans 8:28-30. There we read about the ultimate objective of God, the divine plan and purpose for each believer: "to be conformed to the image of his Son." This is the aim of Christian education, the ultimate objective of the individual's conversion and of the whole process of edification that begins at that time and continues throughout the believer's lifetime on earth (and, perhaps, even in heaven?).

You see, then, what we are discussing is spiritual growth. That is the business of edification. That is what the process of progressive sanctification is all about. The New Testament sets the concept of spiritual growth before us in various terms. In 2 Peter 1:5-7, for example, the process is pictured as a matter of adding Christian graces into one's life to supplement saving faith. But perhaps the most challenging and helpful way the New Testament presents Christian growth is as the fruit of the Spirit.

Ephesians 5:9 tells us that the fruit of the Spirit is seen in all the ways goodness, righteousness, and truth are manifested in a believer's life. Galatians 5:22, 23 are even more specific: "The fruit of the Spirit is love, joy, peace, longsuffering, gentleness, goodness, faith, meekness, temperance." Neither this list of nine (compare the seven in 2 Peter 1:5-7) nor the list of three in Ephesians 5:9 is intended to give us all of the various fruits of the Spirit. These are but samples of the kinds of positive characteristics the Spirit of God is working to produce in the life of the believer.

In fact, all of the Christian graces, all the good things a Christian ought to be, make up the fruit of the Spirit. And in the development of such specific qualities is to be found the precise instrument for measuring spiritual growth. In the development of such qualities of personal character Jesus achieved the ideal of perfect humanity. The goal of our growth is conformity to the image of Christ, measured by His own full stature.

The New Testament gives us a clear picture of the kind of person a Christian ought to be and become: loving, joyous, submissive, self-disciplined, trusting, kind, courteous, pure, patient, impartial, honest, generous, thankful, godly—and so on. The fulness and fruit of the Spirit can be measured in just how well such graces are being developed in the Christian. This means that the very kind of person a believer is must be in a process of transformation toward this ideal, this mature Christ-likeness.

Far too often the insecure and timid person, converted, remains insecure and timid. Or those who are spoiled and self-centered continue to be. The unserious remain so, and likewise those who are too serious. Those who are self-conscious and defensive and tense stay that way. And, tragically, the attainment of the ideal of perfect personhood so clearly demonstrated in Jesus is frustrated. More of the energies of the church must be focused on this problem. Essential to the picture of the functioning church in Ephesians 4:11-16 is the conscious attention that all the members give to the growth of each other, to mutual and reciprocating spiritual edification.

Our heavenly Father has put His Spirit within us for that very purpose. He delights to sniff the sweet fragrance of the flowering Christian life. God is glorified when there is reflected in the church the sparkling beams of the polished gem of Christian maturity. Indeed, men are caused to take note, and there is born in their bosoms the desire to partake, when they see in the saints' lives the ripened fruit of the Spirit.

Subordinate Objectives of the Church

It remains, now for us to discuss some additional objectives of the church, some of the narrower goals that are essential to the larger objective of edification. These, too, are part and parcel to the work of Christian education in the church's life. These might be called *the means of grace*, if one intends, by that, to say that *these are the instruments by which the believer's growth in grace is made to happen.* These are the things the church must attend to if the gracious work of progressive sanctification is to go on in the saints' lives. The fruit of the Spirit, though *His* fruit, cannot be produced apart from the *saints'* use of the means God has made available. (Only, as with edification itself, we must not think of these as *merely* means to an end; each has the right to be considered of value for itself and not just for the part it plays in the edification of the saints.) Each of these will be but briefly discussed as significant objectives of the church. *Many other things could be mentioned,* but four have been chosen as of greatest import.

First, the church exists to proclaim the Word of God. Now it will be readily seen that this objective is of value for itself and is broader than the edification we are discussing here. The proclamation of the Word of God is of critical importance in the work of evangelization, certainly. We might well say that the church has been entrusted with the Word and has the responsibility to share the Word with the world. Withholding the Word from lost men is a sin of staggering proportions.

But the proclamation of the Word of God is also essential in the work of edifying the saints. We have lived with the Bible so long that we take it for granted. We ought not, however, to lose sight of the truth that we hold, in our hands, the very Word of God. Not a word from God, but the Word of God, whole and complete. That Word is God's own authoritative expression of Himself. His very being is somehow supernaturally expressed—communicated—to us in His Word. That Word is truth, that Word is life. To partake of it is to live. To know God's Word is to know Him.

In a very real sense, then, our ministry is a "ministry of the Word" (cf. Acts 6:4). The God of the universe has communicated Himself and His will to us, breathing it out through those holy men who spoke as they were moved (borne) by the Holy Spirit (2 Peter 1:21). The church must break that bread of life to its own, feeding and nourishing them on its milk and its meat (1 Corinthians 3:1, 2; Hebrews 5:12-14; 1 Peter 2:2). That divinely-breathed Word is "profitable for doctrine (teaching), reproof, for correction, for instruction (discipline) in righteousness, that the man of God may be perfect (same word, essentially, as in Ephesians 4:12), thoroughly furnished unto all good works."

In saying the *proclamation* of the Word, we do not limit

the work to formal "preaching," as in a pulpit ministry. Certainly, the pastor's chief work is teaching the Word (Ephesians 4:11). But the proclamation of the Word is not the pastor's work only. Many in the church will give themselves to the study and explanation of the Word. Translations and commentaries are part of the work. Many will teach it, whether to small groups or Sunday school classes or from the pulpit. Some will teach those who must teach others. Many will talk quietly with their neighbors and friends who are unsaved or with their fellow believers. All these things, and more, are essential to the proclamation of the Word. And all the church will sense its unanimous responsibility for, and the part each member plays in, the proclamation of the Word.

Second, the church exists for fellowship, another objective worthy for itself as well as for the part it plays in the edification of the believers within the fellowship. We need a new appreciation, in our time, for the sacredness and value of the fellowship we enter when we are converted.

The creation of this fellowship, this community, is a miraculous and supernatural work. In Ephesians 4:3, Paul calls this fellowship "the unity of the Spirit," meaning that the Holy Spirit is the One who has created this unity, this oneness. When we are saved, the Spirit of God baptizes us into the one body of Christ (Ephesians 4:4, 1 Corinthians 12:13). He ties a knot between us and our fellow believers.

He has not left us to go it alone, and that is desperately important. *We absolutely have to have one another for the successful attaining of the goal of the Christian life.* One of the finest things God has done for us, in salvation, is the uniting of us together in this unique fellowship wherein we are responsible for each other.

Significant, then, is the fact that Paul's exhortation about this "unity of the Spirit" is to *keep*—to preserve, guard—this unity. And no accident is it that the material in Ephesians that follows this key verse (Ephesians 4:3) includes many references to our relationship to each other: forbearing one another (4:2), members of one another (4:25), kind to one another (4:32), forgiving one another (4:32), speaking to one another (5:19), and submitting to one another (5:21). All of this is part of the responsibility we have for one another within the fellowship, "the unity of the Spirit."

So many New Testament passages speak of this that we cannot cover them all here. 1 Thessalonians 5:14, for example, speaks of the responsibility we have, within the fellowship, to "warn them that are unruly" (that is, admonish those that get out of line); to "comfort the feebleminded" (that is, encourage those who are about to run out of steam); to "support the weak" (that is, hold up those who are spiritually infirm); and to "be patient toward all" (that is, bear with them all, whatever their needs and problems).

Hebrews 12:12, 13 has the same concept at its root. Within the fellowship we are responsible for one another so much so that we will "lift up the hands which hang down, and the feeble knees." That is, when some are drooping and stumbling, we must help them stand and encourage them, even (verse 13) remove obstacles from their paths to help them avoid stumbling.

Hebrews 10:24, 25 is especially significant along these lines. The very nature of our fellowship is expressed here, and includes the responsibility to "provoke"—arouse, stimulate—one another (by challenge and example, no doubt) to love and good works; to assemble together regularly; to exhort—encourage—

each other on, and to do this more intensely as "the day" draws nearer.

All this is a part of the nature of the "fellowship" which the church exists to be. We need one another, we are responsible for one another. Therefore, we teach one another, discipline one another, encourage one another, stimulate one another—in short, the body is edifying itself. No effort the church puts forth in "guarding the unity," in promoting closeness and fellowship, is wasted. We must cultivate this sense of responsibility for one another and the submission to one another that marks love. Later in another chapter we will give attention to the pastor's responsibility to cultivate fellowship.

Third, the church exists to minister; or, to put it more correctly, the church exists to help every member develop her or his own capacity for service (ministering). Back to Ephesians 4:11, 12 once more: "He gave . . . pastors and teachers for the perfecting (equipping) of the saints for a work of service." And that service (ministry), itself, aims at building the body. But no matter; even if that service had no final objective of its own, the saints need, for their own good, to minister.

One of the important objectives of the church, then, is to help every member find his own unique place in the overall work of the whole. And that leads not only toward the accomplishing of the purpose of the church as a whole, but toward the full development of the individual believers.

The doctrine that best describes this business of the saints' service is the doctrine of spiritual gifts. The saints' growth is a matter of the fruit of the Spirit; the saints' ministry is a matter of the gifts of the Spirit. Because we will discuss this matter elsewhere in this volume, little needs to be said here. The fact remains that every believer needs an outlet for service, and the church provides that outlet. Every believer needs to feel he has a ministry, and to find something of the meaning of his life in the rendering of that service. The church must help every one discover his part and develop himself for the satisfying performance of that service.

Needing special emphasis is the fact that no two will necessarily play exactly the same part. There are all sorts of service to be rendered in a modern church setting: singing, sweeping, sewing, maintenance, bus work, teaching, preaching, visiting, benevolent work—the list is endless. The primary work of some will be out on the firing line, while others will man the supply lines. Some will be more active in evangelism, others in the work of edification; but all must see their own service in the light of the ultimate purpose of the whole: making disciples, presenting perfect persons to God, building the body.

Fourth, the church exists to worship. Once more, this objective is of its own intrinsic worth, to be valued for itself alone, as well as of importance in the spiritual development of the believer. Christian education has to include this important activity.

Worship might simply be defined as speaking to the Lord. In Ephesians 5:19 we have a direct reference to the worship activity of the church when assembled. Especially is the musical side of that activity described. The church's music, according to this verse, is *both* a "speaking to one another" *and* a "singing . . . unto the Lord." This latter makes it worship. Colossians 3:16, a parallel verse, makes exactly the same point. And both verses go on immediately to tie in "giving thanks always for all things unto God and the Father in the name of our Lord Jesus Christ."

Worship, then, is adoring and praising God, thanking God,

expressing the heart's devotion to God. Every believer needs this singing and praying and praising and thanking, both in his own private worship and in the worship of the gathered fellowship. The maturity of a believer's worship is an unerring indicator of the maturity of his own spiritual development.

But it would be a mistake to promote worship only for the believer's own spiritual growth, as significant as that is. The ultimate truth is that worship is directed to God and it is essential for that reason alone. God deserves our worship. We might even say, in one sense, that He "needs" our worship. To express it better, the one thing He wants from us is our devotion to Him for who He is. Worship is the creature's communication to his Creator, an expression of the joy of knowing God, a glorification of God. The pastor's role in stimulating worship is of concern to us in a later chapter.

Conclusion

We have used this chapter to discuss the overall objective of the church, as the making of disciples or the presenting of complete saints to God, or the building of Christ's body. We have examined the two-fold expression of that one objective in evangelism and edification. And we have examined four subgoals that are essential to all of this, especially to edification. But when we have come, at last, to the matter of worship, we have come to the one ultimate objective that finally displaces them all in importance: the glory of God.

Whether the salvation of sinners or the stablishing of saints, all must give way to this. Ephesians 1:3-14 provides an excellent example of this realization. The passage describes, in dramatic detail, what God has done for us in salvation. In Christ He chose us before the world's foundation, made us acceptable and accepted, holy and blameless (verses 4-6). He brought us—Gentile or Jew—into His one family and put us there in the position of full-fledged sons, with our inheritance already designated and the Spirit of God within us as a guarantee of His earnestness in promising that inheritance (verses 10-14). And for what end has He done this? Running through the marvelous passage is a thrice-repeated refrain, like the chorus after every verse: "To the praise of the glory of his grace" (verses 6, 12, 14).

The church's objective is to win the lost, rescuing hell-deserving sinners, scorched by the flames, to the glorification of a God of mercy and grace who can justly justify the wicked and turn their rebellion into praise. The church's objective is to build up those converted until they have been made to conform to the image of Jesus Christ, ideal and perfect, to the glorification of a God who shapes and molds men from what they had become to what they could be, trophies of His grace. The church's objectives include proclaiming a gracious Word, preserving a gracious fellowship, performing a gracious service, and promoting a gracious worship. And, by all this, the building of the body of Christ, the preparing of a glorious church, without spot or wrinkle, washed in the blood of the Lamb: a Bride for God's Son, perfect and pure, and all by the gracious work of God, whose is all the glory.

And in our worship here we weakly anticipate the ectasy when we will join with all the rest, in perfect accord, in "Blessing, and honour, and glory, and power, unto him that sitteth upon the throne, and unto the Lamb for ever and ever" (Revelation 5:13). Then we will be part of that Bride, the Lamb's wife, descending as the new Jerusalem from heaven, *"Having the glory of God"* (Revelation 21:11).

Discussion Questions

1. Does the author make too great a claim when he says numbers and budgets do not tell us whether either evangelism or edification is primary? If not, what is the significance of church attendance and giving?
2. What word in Ephesians 4:11 supports the author's statement that building up the body of Christ includes evangelism? Can you think of other passages that reflect a similar viewpoint?
3. Is the author being too severe in his criticism when he says, "If sides have to be chosen, if some say that our primary task is evangelism and we only edify the saints to enable them to evangelize, or if others say that a church's purpose is to edify the saints and evangelism is subordinate to that—if any of these things happen, those who are responsible are guilty of sin"? Have they, indeed, "irresponsibly created division and neglected God's imperative"? What implications does your conclusion have for our discussions about the objectives of the church?
4. What does the author mean when he writes, "It is a wicked travesty of the Great Commission to use dollars per soul or souls per hour of work invested as the basis for decisions about when and where to evangelize"? State your reasons for either accepting or rejecting this view.
5. Do you agree with the author when he says "a utilitarian philosophy often twists our concept of the Christian life"? If you do, can you list ways other than that mentioned by the author of the utilitarian philosophy twisting our Christian lives?
6. The author suggests we might continue to be conformed to

the image of Christ even after death. Is there any Scripture to support this suggestion? If so, where?

7. Is it correct to say, as the author does, that "We absolutely have to have one another for the successful attaining of the goal of the Christian life"? Is it not possible for us to mature in Christ on our own? That is to say, if we study, pray, witness, and listen to the Word preached, do we really need other Christians for fellowship?

Chapter V

The Believer And Spiritual Gifts

by Leroy Forlines

Introduction

In our last three chapters, we have been examining the theological foundations of the scope of Christian education. The Old Testament reflects the absolutes of God as well as the wisdom of the Jews. The philosophy of Christian education found in the New Testament is succinctly summarized in the educational practices of Jesus Christ and the principles of education in the New Testament epistles. Naturally, the objectives of evangelism and edification strike at the heart of the scope of educational objectives for the Church. From this theological orientation of the scope of Christian education, we now turn our attention to the people who are of primary importance to education. In this chapter our major concern is with the individual believer who uses his or her gifts of the Spirit to minister for Christ. Later, in other chapters, we will look at people involved as parents, pastors, and staff members.

The subject of spiritual gifts, of course, has gained widespread interest among us today. Interest, at least for many of us, has centered around the charismatic movement with its emphasis on speaking in tongues. Some folks are enthusiastic participants in the movement and feel that there is a baptism of the Holy Spirit that is evidenced by speaking in tongues. With many of these people, speaking in tongues continues to be a part of their Christian life after the experience that they understand to be the initial baptism of the Holy Spirit. Those who testify to this experience believe that it introduces them to a level of Christian living unattainable apart from this experience. While many give glowing testimonies about what speaking in tongues means to them, others of us are quite convinced that this experience is without Scriptural support for the present day.

While much of the attention to spiritual gifts has been in connection with the charismatic movement and its emphasis on tongues, the emphasis on non-sign gifts has also gained widespread attention. Many believers feel that when we discover our spiritual gifts we will gain a deeper satisfaction out of our Christian life and will be more effective in our Christian service. An emphasis on spiritual gifts, it is thought, will cause more of us to participate in the ministry of the church and will create a mutual respect among us as fellow believers. This would contribute to a stronger sense of fellowship within the church as we have just seen in our previous chapter. While no one challenges the fact that the Bible does teach that the Holy Spirit has given different gifts to believers, all of us do not give the same stress to the subject of gifts. Some of us feel that a stress on gifts leads to a restructuring of the local church and the church services. Others of us believe that the emphasis on spiritual gifts can be given without significant changes in the organization of churches and the order of church services.

The widespread emphasis on both the sign gifts and non-sign gifts along with the conflicting opinions on the subject make it important that we study the subject of spiritual gifts. The major concern of our study will be on the non-sign gifts; however, the interest in sign gifts demands that we give attention to sign gifts, too.

The Nature of Personal Relationships

Since God is personal and man is personal, it is important that as a background context for discussing spiritual gifts brief attention should be given to the nature of personal relationships. A person is one who thinks, feels, and acts. The actions of a person are at least to some extent his own. A person is never purely passive in his own actions. He may be acted upon, but he is also active and his action is to some extent his own action. He is never completely taken over, so far as the actions of his personality are concerned, by another person or force. For such to happen would be a violation of his personality. God will not violate the personality of man in His relationship to man. Man is a personal being by the design of God.

Before proceeding further, we need to distinguish between personal relationships and mechanical relationships. Mechanical relationships are described in terms of cause and effect. Influence and response is a better way of describing personal relationships. A cause guarantees an effect. An influence contributes to the possibility of a desired response, but it does not guarantee the response. We may sometimes speak of cause and effect when we refer to personal relationships, but we are using the terms loosely and mean influence and response. When we hit a nail square on the head, with a hammer, it causes it to go into the board. When we preach to people, we appeal to them for a response; we may or may not get the desired response.

Man is a personal being. None of God's dealings with man violate his personality. We may talk about a Spirit-controlled life, but we are not using the word controlled in a mechanical sense. The Holy Spirit does not control a person in terms of cause and effect. If He did, man would be a puppet, not a person. The Holy Spirit influences, enables, and strengthens, but all of the actions of a believer are his own actions. Man is never more personal than when in a right relationship with God. A right relationship with God brings a person to the highest development of his potential as a thinking, feeling, acting being.[1]

The Sign Gifts

According to 1 Corinthians 14:22, speaking in tongues was a sign gift. Based on the use of the word *sign* in the New Testament, we would also conclude that the gifts of miracles and healing would also be sign gifts. The interpretation of tongues would be a sign gift and was an essential accompaniment of the exercise of the gift of tongues in public worship (1 Corinthians 14:28).

Since the gifts of miracles, healing, tongues, and the interpretation of tongues were sign gifts, it will be in order to study the significance of signs in the New Testament. There are three Greek words that are used to describe those supernatural works which we designate miracle. These are *dunamis, teras,* and *semeion. Dunamis* describes the event as a manifestation of Divine power. *Teras* describes the event as being an extraordinary event that has been observed. The observer reacts with wonder and amazement. *Semeion* describes the event as having theological significance. It is designed to reveal the presence and nature of God and to authenticate the one performing the miracle and his message as having Divine approval. *Teras* does not appear in the New Testament without being accompanied by *semeion*. At times these two are also accompanied by *dunamis*.[2]

It is important for the individual believer who is earnest about using his gifts for God to recognize the significance of miraculous events in the New Testament. They are clearly viewed as *semeion* (signs). John 20:30-31 are instructive concerning the purpose of Jesus' miracles: "And many other signs truly did Jesus in the presence of his disciples, which are not written in this book: But these are written, that ye might believe that Jesus is the Christ, the Son of God; and that believing you might have life through his name."

John gives special stress on the sign value of Jesus' miracles. They were designed to show God's approval of Jesus as an aid for believing in Jesus. It is interesting to observe that *semeion* is the word in John that is translated miracle in every occurrence of the word *miracle* in John's Gospel. It is also the word that is translated *sign* when it occurs in John's Gospel. The meaning is clearer when we use the word *signs* where it is translated miracle. This shows the stress that John gives to the sign value of Jesus' miracles.

Acts 2:22 is also to the point concerning the purpose of Jesus' miracles. It reads: "Ye men of Israel, hear these words; Jesus of Nazareth, a man approved of God among you by miracles and wonders and signs, which God did by him in the midst of you, as ye yourselves also know." The results of Jesus' miracles were clearly visible and gave evidence of God's approval.

Miraculous events also bore witness to the truth of the gospel when those who heard Jesus went out and preached.

With reference to the so great salvation, the writer of Hebrews explains, "which at the first began to be spoken by the Lord, and was confirmed unto us by them that heard him. God also bearing them witness both with signs and wonders, and divers miracles, and gifts of the Holy Ghost, according to his own will." The word from which gifts is translated is not the same word that is most frequently translated gifts. It means distributions. However, it is clear that distributions refer to gifts. In this passage we see these gifts as clearly having the value of a sign. Not all gifts have sign value, but the ones of a miraculous nature do.

According to 2 Corinthians 12:12 the ministry of the apostle was accompanied by miracles as signs to authenticate their apostleship. Paul said, "Truly the signs of an apostle were wrought among you in all patience, in signs, and wonders, and mighty deeds" (see also Romans 15:18-19).

On the day of Pentecost, Peter refers to a prophecy of Joel to explain that the unusual things which people witnessed that day were signs (Acts 2:19). This would include the speaking of tongues on that day (Acts 2:4-11). The people from other countries were utterly astounded to hear these disciples speaking to them in their own language. Peter explained that this unusual happening was a sign. It was a sign of the truth of Jesus Christ, the salvation which He had provided, and of the coming of the Holy Spirit for a new relationship with believers.

The sign value of the miracles of the Book of Acts is beyond doubt if we study the use of the word *semeion* (sign) in the Book of Acts. Other than the places already mentioned, it occurs in the following places and is translated "signs" (Acts 2:43; 4:30; 5:12; 7:36; 8:13; and 14:3). It occurs in the following places and is translated "miracle" (Acts 4:16, 22; 6:8;

8:6, 13; and 15:12). A study of these passages makes it unquestionably clear that the miraculous occurred in the early church to confirm the truth of the gospel.

This survey of the purpose of the miraculous in the New Testament should make it unquestionably clear that miracles did not occur in the New Testament simply for the enjoyment of the beneficiary of the miracle. Neither were the miracles simply God's response to the faith of the individual miracle worker. They had a sign value. As individual believers, then, we have no reason for expecting miracles to continue in plentitude apart from the need of the sign value of the miracles.

As we have observed, there were three basic reasons for the miraculous signs in the New Testament: a) they were performed by Jesus as a sign of God's approval upon Him, His claims, and His message; b) they were performed by the apostles as a sign of their apostleship; c) they were performed by the apostles and a few others as a sign of the truth of the New Testament revelation of the gospel and the new relationship of the Holy Spirit to believers.

In the light of the sign value of miracles in the New Testament, what expectations should the individual believer have about miracles today? We rule out the first reason given above because Jesus is not on earth today and He has already been established as the Son of God and Savior of those who believe. We rule out the second reason because there is no officer in the church for which a miraculous sign is required to attest the right of a person to fill that office (See the requirements of bishops or pastors and deacons in 1 Timothy 3:2-13 and Titus 1:5-9). We rule out the third reason because the gospel has already been established and has 2000 years of history behind it. If there is an exception at this point, it would be in places where the gospel is now being taken for the first time. If the purpose of the miraculous as it occurred in the New Testament is any clue to God's purpose in working miracles, to say the least, we would not expect them to be very plentiful in our day. We can say the same about the sign gifts which are miraculous in kind.

Baptism of the Holy Spirit

At least brief attention should be given to the matter of the baptism of the Holy Spirit as it is tied in with the gift of tongues. Those in the tongues movement speak of a baptism of the Holy Spirit which is said to be subsequent to conversion and evidenced by speaking in tongues. This teaching is based solely on the Book of Acts. There are only three instances of speaking in tongues in the Book of Acts: a) the day of Pentecost (Acts 2:4-11); b) the occasion when Peter preached to the Gentiles for the first time (Acts 10:44-48); c) the time when Paul baptized those who had only known John's baptism (Acts 19:2-6).

We find only two mentions of baptism with the Holy Spirit in the Book of Acts. The first is Jesus' prediction of what would take place on the day of Pentecost (Acts 1:5). The second is Peter's reference back to what happened when the Gentiles received the Holy Spirit (Acts 11:16). He is referring back to Acts 10:44-48. In both of these cases, reference is made to these occasions as being a fulfillment of the prophecy of John the Baptist with regard to the baptism with the Holy Spirit.

Since these are the only two references to a baptism with

the Holy Spirit recorded in Acts, it is important that we understand them. Let us first look at the occasion in Acts 10:44-48. Was this experience at the time of conversion or subsequent to conversion? It is obvious that it was at the time of conversion. "While Peter yet spake these words, the Holy Ghost fell on all them which heard the word" (Acts 10:44). This occasion cannot be understood as baptism with the Holy Spirit subsequent to conversion. Since it was simultaneous with conversion, it is obvious that it could not have been subsequent to the initial receiving of the Holy Spirit. It was the initial receiving of the Holy Spirit. This leaves only one more occasion to consider.

It is true that those who had already been converted were baptized with the Holy Spirit on the day of Pentecost. However, we need to examine this case more closely before we say that the Bible teaches that there is a baptismal experience subsequent to conversion for believers. The day of Pentecost is unique in the history of the church. There has never been and never will be a repetition of that day. It marked the beginning of the relationship of the Holy Spirit to the believer as we now experience Him. It was impossible for those who were saved before Pentecost to have received the Holy Spirit in the same sense that they received Him on the day of Pentecost. This being true, there can be no present day doctrine of a baptism of the Holy Spirit subsequent to conversion based on what happened on the day of Pentecost to those who had been saved prior to that time.

The only two occurrences in Acts of a baptism with the Holy Spirit have been examined. It is obvious that no support for a baptism of the Holy Spirit for us subsequent to conversion can be extracted from either Acts 2 or Acts 10. In Acts 2, it was the first time any believer could have had such an experience because it was the beginning of the Holy Spirit's ministry as it is in the present age. In Acts 10, the people were baptized with the Holy Spirit at the time of conversion.

There is only one other reference to a baptism with or by the Holy Spirit other than the prophetic reference of John the Baptist. This reference is found in 1 Corinthians 12:13. The expression in the Greek is similar to that in Acts 1:5 and 11:16. The preposition that is translated *with* in Acts 1:5 and 11:16 is translated *by* in 1 Corinthians 12:13. This means that the expressions are more alike in the Greek than the English. The main difference is the addition of the words "into one body" in 1 Corinthians 12:13. These additional words make some people think that in this verse it is a baptism into the body of Christ by the Holy Spirit. This is thought to be different from the experience in Acts where the baptism is also called being filled with the Holy Spirit. Many people think the meaning in all three places is the same. It is not necessary for us to decide which interpretation of 1 Corinthians 12:13 is correct in order to see what bearing it has on whether it supports the idea of a baptism with the Holy Spirit after conversion. Whatever Paul meant by, "For by one Spirit are we all baptized into one body," one thing is clear. It was an experience in which all believers had shared. That being true 1 Corinthians 12:13 cannot be used to lend support to the idea of a baptism with the Holy Spirit after conversion. If the doctrine cannot be supported from Acts 1:5; 11:16; and 1 Corinthians 12:13, we cannot find support for it in the New Testament.

The two occurrences in Acts which are referred to as a baptism with the Holy Spirit are two of the three references in Acts where there is a record of tongues speaking. Let us look at the third reference and see if a common ground can be found for all three occurrences of tongues speaking.

In Acts 19, the people under consideration had been obedient to the preaching of John the Baptist (Acts 19:3). They had not heard about the fact that Jesus had already provided redemption and that the Holy Spirit had come. As soon as they did, they believed and Paul baptized them with water. Immediately they received the Holy Spirit and spoke in tongues (Acts 19:4-6). This was the first time that their faith had embraced the crucified and risen Lord and Savior. It was the first time it had been possible for them to receive the Holy Spirit as we now experience Him.

Having examined these three passages where it is said that they spoke in tongues, it is obvious that all three instances have one thing in common. On each occasion, it was the first time that the people had received the Holy Spirit. It was this original reception of the Holy Spirit that was attested by the sign of tongues speaking.

It should be observed that there is a clear case in Acts of a group who received the Holy Spirit after conversion. When Philip preached in Samaria there were many who believed and were baptized (Acts 8:12). They did not receive the Holy Spirit until Peter and John went and prayed that they might receive the Holy Spirit (Acts 8:15-17). This was the original receiving of the Holy Spirit on their part not a baptism with the Holy Spirit after they had received the Holy Spirit.

The tongues speaking in Acts attested the original receiving of the Holy Spirit, not an experience with the Holy Spirit subsequent to the original receiving of the Holy Spirit. According to the interpretation of Acts 1:5 and 11:16, the baptism with the Holy Spirit refers to the receiving of the Holy

Spirit. Romans 8:9 tells us, "Now if any man have not the Spirit of Christ, he is none of his." The context makes it clear that the Spirit of Christ is the Holy Spirit. If we do not have the Holy Spirit, we are not believers. If tongues is required as evidence for being baptized with the Holy Spirit, it would be required as evidence for salvation since no one is saved who does not have the Holy Spirit. This cannot be. Not even those who advocate tongues claim that only those who speak in tongues are saved.

How do we cope with this problem? We view the Book of Acts as dealing with a transition period. It was a period in which the gospel was being established. Many new truths were being preached. Many practical changes were being made as Christians came to know what it meant to be delivered from the law to the New Covenant. This was a time which called for signs to indicate that God's approval was on what was taking place.

During the time that the new relationship of the Holy Spirit to God's people was being introduced, the sign of speaking in tongues was used as a sign that God was in what was taking place. After this new relationship with the Holy Spirit was fully established, the need of a sign to attest to the reality of the experience was no longer needed. In Romans 8:9 Paul is giving us the permanent doctrine of the Church. There is not the slightest indication that tongues were to be a sign of receiving the Holy Spirit after the transition period was completed.

When the transition period was completed, the question of when the Holy Spirit is received was also settled. In Acts 8 He was received after conversion. These people needed the impressiveness of having Peter and John come and pray and lay hands on them (Acts 8:14-17) because of the newness of the experience. Romans 8:9 gives us the permanent doctrine of the church. We receive the Holy Spirit at conversion.

The Filling of the Holy Spirit

If we cannot find an experience in Scripture subsequent to conversion and the initial receiving of the Holy Spirit by the name of baptism with the Holy Spirit that is evidenced by tongues speaking, what about one called being filled with the Holy Spirit? There is no once and for all filling with the Holy Spirit in the New Testament. Peter and John were among those who were filled with the Holy Spirit on the day of Pentecost (Acts 2:4). Both of these were in the number that were filled with the Holy Spirit in Acts 4:31. This was the second time for John that he partook of an experience referred to as being filled with the Holy Spirit according to the account given in Acts. It was the third time for Peter. In Acts 4:8 it reads, "Then Peter, filled with the Holy Ghost, said unto them . . . " The word filled in the Greek is an aorist passive participle. The meaning is that Peter, after having been filled, spoke. He had received a filling immediately prior to speaking.

The next mention of a person being filled with the Holy Spirit is Acts 9:17 where Paul was filled with the Holy Spirit. In Acts 13:9 Paul was filled again. "Then Saul . . . filled with the Holy Ghost, set his eyes on him." This is another case of an aorist participle. Paul had been filled with the Holy Spirit immediately prior to setting his eyes on Elymas the sorcerer. The only other occasion in Acts where it refers to being filled with the Holy Spirit is Acts 13:52. Paul was in the group that was said to be filled. This is the third recorded instance where Paul was filled with the Holy Spirit.

The above listing is a complete listing of the occurrences in

Acts where the word *filled* is used to describe the experience of a person with the Holy Spirit. It is quite evident that in no instance does it describe an experience subsequent to the initial receiving of the Holy Spirit that is to be a once and for all experience. One would gather that it could happen many times. An interpretation of the use of the word *filled* in Acts offers no help to those who seek to establish the idea of a special experience evidenced by speaking in tongues after the initial receiving of the Holy Spirit. After the Book of Acts, there is only one reference to being filled with the Holy Spirit. This is in Ephesians 5:18, "And be not drunk with wine, wherein is excess; but be filled with the Spirit." The word for be filled in the Greek is a present imperative and means, "Be ye being filled with the Spirit." This calls for continuous submission to the Holy Spirit to be filled by Him. It suggests no idea of some special experience after conversion that a person should seek for filling with the Holy Spirit whether evidenced by tongues or not.

The Sign Gifts in 1 Corinthians 12-14

Up to this point, we have noted that the Bible does not support the viewpoint that there is a baptism with the Holy Spirit subsequent to conversion that is evidenced by speaking with tongues. If this fact were adhered to, the Scriptural truth alone would bring a near death blow to the so-called charismatic movement. However, brief attention must be given to the sign gifts in 1 Corinthians 12-14. As has already been observed these are gifts of miracles, healings, tongues, and the interpretation of tongues.

Tongues is referred to as a sign gift in 1 Corinthians 14:22. That the gift of miracles, healings, and the interpretation of tongues would be sign gifts is clear from their miraculous nature. We have already discussed the question of the occurrence of signs today in the earlier treatment of the subject of signs in this study.

Miracles did not just occur in Scripture. They were signs. There can be no reason to expect the miraculous gifts to occur in our day unless there is a need for signs. If this line of reasoning were followed, to say the least, sign gifts would be extremely rare if they would occur at all. Certainly, they are not to be interpreted as necessary signs of deep spirituality. They never were. Neither are they necessary consequences of a strong faith. They came on the scene in the early church not as a result of deep spirituality or a super faith. Rather, they happened in keeping with the purposes of God to give signs of approval to the apostles, the new truth of the New Testament revelation, and the new experience with the Holy Spirit. The miraculous is not a necessary sign of spirituality. Signs of spirituality in the church today are the salvation of souls and the manifestation of the fruit of the Holy Spirit in the lives of believers. As individual believers, then, we would not expect the Holy Spirit to endow us with sign gifts today.

Non-Sign Gifts

The non-sign gifts are those gifts that are not miraculous in nature. For that reason they have no sign value. Therefore, there is no question concerning their continuation in the church today. While our interest in sign gifts is primarily negative, since we have concluded that the need for their occurrence today does not exist as it did in the day of the New Testament, our interest in non-sign gifts is positive since they are a part of the church today. It is these gifts that each of us as believers needs to understand and utilize when we are endowed with them.

Before looking at the variety and purpose of non-sign gifts, we need to specify exactly what it is that we as believers need to be using for God. The word that is most frequently translated "gift" when referring to spiritual gifts is the word *charisma. Charis* is the word for grace. *Charisma* refers to the gift as being a concrete manifestation of God's grace. The word *spiritual* denotes the nature of the gift and the fact that the Holy Spirit is the one who bestows and energizes the gift.

Charisma is used only one time in the New Testament outside the writings of Paul (see 1 Peter 4:10). *Charisma* is not restricted in its use to what is referred to technically as spiritual gifts.

In Romans 5:15-16, *charisma* refers to the gift of justification. In Romans 6:23 it refers to the gift of eternal life. In Romans 1:11 it is debated whether Paul used *charisma* to refer to spiritual gift in the technical sense or whether he simply meant that he wanted to impart some blessing to the people that would contribute to their spiritual stedfastness. In any case the context does not help us in elaborating the doctrine of spiritual gifts. Romans 11:29 sheds no light on the subject since it merely says that God does not repent concerning His gifts to His people. In 1 Corinthians 1:7 *charisma* appears to refer to gift in a broad sense, but if it should refer to spiritual gifts in the restricted sense, not enough is said to shed light on the subject. 1 Corinthians 7:7 makes use of *charisma* to refer to the help of God enabling a person to remain unmarried without burning with lust. In 2 Corinthians 1:11 the gift is general in nature and makes no contribution to our subject.

The occurrences of the word *charisma* that are not mentioned above are all dealing with the subject of spiritual gifts in the limited sense. These are Romans 12:6; 1 Corinthians 12:4, 9, 28, 30, 31; 1 Timothy 4:14; 2 Timothy 1:6; and 1 Peter 4:10.

While *charisma* is the word that is used in most places where spiritual gifts are under discussion, it is not the only word that is used for gift in such cases. In Ephesians 3:7 Paul attributes the fact that he was a minister to "the gift of the grace of God." The word for gift in the verse is *dorea*. This same word is used in Ephesians 4:7 where the context as it is developed in verses 8-11 shows that the subject is spiritual gifts. The word *doma* is used one time to refer to spiritual gifts (Ephesians 4:8). In Ephesians, by the use of *dorea* and *doma*, there is no reason to believe that Paul means anything essentially different than he would if he had used the word *charisma*. In Hebrews 2:4 the word *merismos* is translated gift. While the word *gifts* is an acceptable translation, in Hebrews 2:4, the basic thought is distributions. The emphasis is on the fact that the Holy Spirit was in charge of the distribution.

From the above observations, we draw the following conclusions. (a) Spiritual gifts issue forth from God's grace, are spiritual in nature, and are bestowed by the Holy Spirit. (b)

Charisma is the word most often used to refer to spiritual gifts in the restricted sense; however, it is not the only word that is so used. Also, *charisma* is used in the New Testament sense to refer to what can rightly be called a gift of God. Only the context determines whether *charisma* is used in the restricted sense usually meant by our reference to spiritual gifts or in a broader sense. (c) Since the Greek word *dorea* and *doma* are used as well as *charisma* with reference to the subject of spiritual gifts, it appears that the English word *gift* serves quite well when talking about the subject of spiritual gifts. (d) There is no special meaning involved in the word *charisma* that cannot be gathered from the word *gift* when the context is considered. (e) There are three major passages that deal with the non-sign gifts. These are Romans 12:3-8; 1 Corinthians 12; and Ephesians 4:8-11. First Timothy 4:14; 2 Timothy 1:6 and 1 Peter 4:10 add some to our understanding of the subject.

In each of the major passages given to the subject of gifts, Paul gives attention to the fact that among believers there is a variety of gifts. In Romans 12:6, Paul speaks of gifts as "differing according to the grace that is given to us." All gifts come from the same reservoir of grace, but they differ as to their nature from one person to another. 1 Corinthians 12:4 and the basic thought as developed through verse 8 lay stress on the fact that different people have different gifts. Ephesians 4:11 makes it clear that as a result of the differences in the gifts received some were to be apostles, some were to be prophets, some were to be evangelists, and some were to be pastors and teachers. The Greek construction requires us to understand pastors and teachers to be referring to the same person, as some say pastor-teacher.

The idea of diversity in 1 Corinthians 12:4-6 is connected

with three different words. Each of these are different aspects of the same thing. These words are *gift* (verse 4), *administrations* (verse 5), and *operations* (verse 6). The word translated "administration" is most frequently translated "ministry." The exact form of the word translated "operations" appears only one other time in the New Testament. In 1 Corinthians 12:10 it is translated "working" with reference to the gift of "working miracles." It can be translated "operation," "working," "work," "activity," "energy," and so on. Some take the reference to be Divine activity. Others understand the reference to be to human activity. Since gifts in verse 4 and ministries in verse 5 relate to the Christian, it appears that it would be better to identify the activity of verse 6 with the Christian. Taking this approach, that under consideration is called a gift because it is God given. It is a ministry because it has service as its aim and responsibility. It is called activity because work is involved in performing the ministry. It is important to observe that all of these are plural-gifts, ministries, and activities. God is the author of this plurality or diversity.

In 1 Corinthians 12:7 Paul says with reference to the bestowal of gifts by the Holy Spirit, "But the manifestation of the Spirit is given to every man to profit withal." The meaning of that which is translated "to profit withal" is for good or for profit. The gift makes the individual believer profitable to the church. The gifts of believers are to be manifested in ministries (1 Corinthians 12:7). These ministries are designed for the good of the church. According to 1 Peter 4:10, gifts are to result in ministering to one another as Christians.

In Ephesians 4:11 and 12 Paul deals with the purpose of what we will call office gifts. This group is what we might refer to as the ordained personnel in the church. Verse 11 makes it clear that each person holds the office that he does because it is a gift of God.

It is not necessary for us at this time to deal with the question of the exact nature of the gifts in Ephesians 4:11 or whether they are all continuing in the church today. It is enough to observe that there is a diversity of such gifts and that they have a purpose. The purpose is "For the perfecting of the saints, for the work of the ministry . . . ." The word for perfecting means "equipping." It is not translated from the Greek word for perfect that is most frequently used in the New Testament which means complete or mature. The word that is translated "perfecting" is closely related to the word that is translated "perfect" in 2 Timothy 3:17. The verse explains the word as meaning fully equipped for every good work, or fully equipped for service.

Based on the view that the Greek word for perfecting means equipped for service, it is the purpose of the office gifts to equip the laity for service. This meaning is given further support by connecting the equipping of the saints with "for the work of the ministry." Individual believers, therefore, are to be equipped for ministry of service in the work of the church. The purpose of this is "for the edifying of the body of Christ." The purpose of the ministry of individual believers is to edify the church spiritually. However, it would certainly be clear from the whole New Testament that the ministry of the laity in the church should also involve an outreach ministry to win sinners to Christ.

Perhaps we should make an observation at this point. God has given to the church people with different office gifts to contribute to the equipping of individual believers for the work of the ministry. It is important that Christians benefit from the ministry of people with different gifts, thus different emphases. It takes the ministry of people with different gifts to minister to the overall needs of Christians.

There are many people in the church that do not possess an office gift. However, it is important that we observe that *every* person has a gift (1 Corinthians 12:7). Every person has a gift that will enable him to contribute to the needs of the church.

The Practical Implications of the Doctrine of Gifts

As we have pointed out above, every believer has a gift or gifts. This means that every person in the church has a ministry. The nature of the individual believer's ministry is determined by his gift. Peter says that we are to minister to one another according to our gift (1 Peter 4:10). The main stress of Paul in Romans 12:3-8 is that we have different gifts and that we are to minister according to our gifts. In 1 Corinthians 3:5 Paul explains that he and Apollos ministered "as the Lord gave to every man." In verse 6 he explained that he planted and Apollos watered.

There is nothing more frustrating to a sincere Christian than to feel a special obligation to minister in an area and to be unfruitful in spite of his most sincere efforts because he is not ministering in the area of his gifts. Many Christians can be very fruitful in one area while their efforts in other areas either prove to be unfruitful or render very meager results. God has not intended that we all fit into the same mold. One of the most important things that a believer can do is to find his real identity as it is reflected in a proper understanding of his gifts.

One of the greatest things that can happen to us as Christians is to decide to be what God has made us in terms of gifts and abilities. We will learn to be ourselves and not somebody else. We will be happier, more at ease within ourselves, and more fruitful after we decide to be stewards of our gifts and to minister according to our gifts. Many sincere Christians are "tied in knots" by trying to be somebody else.

Having a proper understanding of our gifts is intended to help us have a proper attitude toward ourselves. In 1 Corinthians 12:15-20 Paul tells us that no member of our physical body should develop an inferiority complex or feel a sense of worthlessness because it is not some other member of the body. The foot, the hand, the ear, the eye, and the nose all have important roles in the complete functioning of our body. We are handicapped by the absence of any of these members. Paul uses the members of the body to illustrate how every believer with his gifts makes an important contribution to the church.

There are many things that go on around a church upon which we place very little value until they are undone. The importance of having someone to open the church is seldom realized until several arrive one day and they cannot get in until someone locates a set of keys. The importance of the work of one who sets the thermostats is not realized until people are either too hot or too cold. The importance of the janitorial work in a church is not realized until it is left undone one day. Then, everyone is embarrassed.

Other things could be added to the things listed above, such as the work of the ushers, the time-consuming work of the church treasurer, and so forth. Blessed is the church that has people who are faithful and effective in these areas. No church will ever experience significant growth without having people who are faithful and efficient in these positions. Yet, many people serve well in these areas and similar areas without feeling any real sense of worth and satisfaction. Those who serve well in any area should receive a sense of satisfaction within themselves and the church should recognize the value of these services.

In 1 Corinthians 12:21-25, Paul explains that no part of the human body is sufficient if it be alone. As important as the eye is, it "cannot say to the hand, I have no need of thee." As important as the head may be, it cannot say to "the feet, I have no need of you." Just as no part of the human body should look condescendingly upon another member of the body, so a person with one gift in the church should not look condescendingly upon a member with another.

It is very important that we have the right attitude toward each other when each person is ministering according to his gift. The church needs the ministry of people with different gifts. The fruit of some ministries are more measurable than others. For example, the quantitative growth of a church can be measured better than the qualitative growth. That is to say, it is easier to determine the number of people who accept Christ as their Savior than it is to determine the spiritual growth of those who are already Christians. While one can be measured more easily than the other, neither should intimidate the other, nor be intimidated by the other. The evangelistic ministry of the church which measures success in terms of quantity and the edifying ministry of the church which measures results in terms of quality need each other. If you cut one, both bleed. Neither can exist in good health without the other.

The church must be aggressively evangelistic. The church must take aggressive steps to ground new converts and to edify all the members. In a sense it may be said that each is the by-product of the other. However, neither will exist in full health as a mere by-product of the other. Each must be made a goal of the church. Some will contribute more to evangelization. Others will contribute more to edification, but each should have a concern for the success of the other. When gifts are properly understood, they lead to a mutual respect and a mutual concern for one another (1 Corinthians 12:23-26). Paul explains that in the human body there is harmony and concern among the members. He explains, "And whether one member suffer, all the members suffer with it; or one member be honoured, all the members rejoice with it" (verse 26). Paul is implying that this is the attitude that members with different gifts should have one to another in the church. When this is the case, harmony prevails rather than schism (verses 24-25).

Discovering Your Gifts

If we as individual believers are to minister according to our gifts, this raises the question of how a person discovers his gifts. First, let it be said that the subject of gifts in the Bible is meant to encourage rather than to discourage. If people become "tied in knots" concerning the discovery of their gifts, that would defeat one of the purposes of gifts. For a person who is sincerely dedicated to serving God, there should be no great difficulty involved in knowing what he needs to know about his gifts.

We are convinced that there are certain ministries, like the pastoral ministry, that are to be entered only if a person has received a Divine call. It would be apparent that if a person has received a Divine call to a particular service that he would have the gifts essential to that work. This does not mean that all people who are called to a particular work have the same gifts, but it does mean that they would have gifts essential to the work.

Concerning the discovery of particular gifts both on the part of the clergy and the laity, a person begins with the opportunities for service that are available to him. When he labors in the area of his gifts, it would be expected that he would be more fruitful than in laboring outside his gifts. Also, a person should have a sense of ease and satisfaction when laboring in the area of his gifts. If a person feels awkward in an area of work after spending a reasonable length of time in it, it would appear that he is laboring outside the area of his gifts. If his efforts are unfruitful after a reasonable time, it would appear that he is laboring outside the area of his gifts. Yet, we should be careful in drawing the conclusion that we are unfruitful in view of the fact that fruitfulness is not always easily measured. Also, there are some situations in which fruit comes slowly.

While a person should be able to make judgments regarding his gifts, spiritually-minded people can also be helpful in the discovery of the gifts of another. When other Christians feel that a person functions well in an area, that is an indication that he is likely gifted in that area.

While a person can be expected to be more fruitful when ministering in the area of his gifts, there should be no waiting on the sideline until the gifts are discovered. There is no harm in participating in an area of work for which one has not received a gift. The commands of Scripture require us at times to involve ourselves in things for which we have not received a gift. For example, each of us should be a steward of his opportunities to witness to sinners. However, the gifts of some people would involve them more in soul-winning than someone else who may have the responsibility without the gift. All Christians should be prepared to do some explaining of the Bible to others, but a person with the gift of teaching would be more involved in such a ministry. The very fact that a person is heavily involved in one kind of ministry will subtract some from what he can do in other ministries.

Types of Gifts

A brief look at the gifts mentioned in the New Testament will be of some value in determining one's gifts. There are different ways of categorizing gifts. Our division is as follows: office gifts, speaking gifts, and service gifts. Our discussion at this point will be in a general sense. In a later chapter, we will apply this method of analysis to the church staff.

Office gifts include apostles, prophets, evangelists, and the pastor-teachers (Ephesians 4:11 and 1 Corinthians 12:28). Those entering these works do so because they have received a call. It appears that we no longer have apostles. They had a very important place in the earliest days of the church. They spoke at times under inspiration. Some wrote under inspiration. God revealed truth through them and wrought signs through them.

We do not have prophets today as an exact equivalent of the Biblical prophet. Biblical prophets received revelations from God. We do not have prophets in that sense today. Prophets had a corrective ministry. They had a message of guilt, judgment, and hope. They brought the message and power of God on a situation. Prophets would not exist as a separate office, but there are people who have a ministry that is similar to the prophetic ministry apart from the idea of receiving revelations.

Evangelists, from what we can gather, means about the same in the New Testament that it does today. The pastor-teacher would be the same as our pastor today. Pastor means shepherd and parallels the work of the pastor with that of a shepherd caring for his sheep. Teacher stresses the fact that the pastor should be a teacher (1 Timothy 3:2).

Speaking gifts are the gifts of prophecy, teaching, the word of knowledge, the word of wisdom, and exhortation (Romans 12:6-8 and 1 Corinthians 12:8). Some of the office gifts would also be speaking gifts, but they have already been dealt with above. All of the gifts referred to as speaking gifts and serving gifts can be experienced by the average believer or layman.

What has been said about prophets as it relates to today would be applicable to prophecy. Teaching and the word of knowledge would be closely related. The word of knowledge could apply to private conversation as well as group teaching. The word of wisdom refers to the ability to make good practical judgments and communicate them to others. Exhortation refers to the ability to encourage.

The serving gifts are ministering, helps, giving, showing mercy, faith, discerning spirits, ruling, and governments (Romans 12:7-8 and 1 Corinthians 12:9, 10, and 28). Ministry and helps are usually considered to be the same gift. The reference is lending various forms of assistance. The gift of giving refers to giving money. All are to give, but some have been blessed in a special way to give. The gift of showing mercy refers to being gifted at showing compassion to those in need or those who have a problem. The gift of faith refers to the gift to act upon faith. This is a gift that projects some people into ventures of faith. Others may be supposed to act more in accord with sound judgment based on known factors. The gift of discerning spirits refers to the ability to discern dangerous trends, the ability to detect heresy, and the ability to detect demonic powers. The gifts of ruling and government refer to the same gift. It is the ability to be effective in administrative roles. It is an ability that achieves its purpose in the framework of church government and with a deep appreciation for the concerns and needs of the people.

Some list hospitality as a gift based on 1 Peter 4:9-10. It is obvious that the list of gifts does not propose to be complete. They illustrate the main areas where gifts operate.

Many people perform many of the ministries related to the gifts without really realizing that it is a vital ministry of the church. This is especially true of the serving gifts. A realization of gifts helps the members of the church to see more clearly the value of what they are doing and what others are doing.

Conclusion

Though gifts are bestowed by God, they are not bestowed fully developed. On the one side they are a Divine gift. On the other side they take on the form of a human ability. As such they can and should be developed through education, training, and experience. The possession of a gift does not guarantee the proper use of that gift. Gifts must be disciplined by the principles taught in Scripture.

We need to have an awareness of the Scriptural teaching on gifts as individual believers. Such an understanding will prove to be a benefit to the individual and the church as a whole. We need an awareness in this sphere, but not an obsession. The doctrine of gifts is a way of involving more people in the ministry of the church and cultivating a mutual respect for the diversity of ministries. This can be done without changing the governmental structure of the church and without making significant changes in the order of the services. When properly applied, an understanding of spiritual gifts will strengthen every ministry in the church. Both the evangelization of the church and the edification of the church will be strengthened when we minister according to our gifts.

Discussion Questions

1. Is the argument sound that says, "If the purpose of the miraculous as it occurred in the New Testament is any clue to God's purpose in working miracles, to say the least, we would not expect them to be very plentiful in our day"? What counter arguments would you expect to hear to this statement? Are they sound?

2. What does the author appear to be arguing for when he states, "It is important that Christians benefit from the ministry of people with different gifts, thus different emphases. It takes the ministry of people with different gifts to minister to the overall needs of Christians"? What are some practical applications of this thought?

3. The author suggests, "God has not intended that we all fit into the same mold." Are you as certain of this as he appears to be? Why?

4. Is there anything a local church can do to make sure that those who serve well in any area of service receive a sense of satisfaction for their service? If so, what?

5. Does the fact that the Scriptures seem to assume Christians will discover their gifts support the author's statement that, "For a person who is sincerely dedicated to serving God, there should be no great difficulty involved in knowing what he needs to know about his gifts"? If not, why?

6. What might the author have in mind when he writes, "The possession of a gift does not guarantee the proper use of that gift. Gifts must be disciplined by the principles taught in Scriptures"? Do you disagree with him? Why or why not?

7. Some people argue a great deal about whether a person can have more than one gift. Do you think this question is a crucial one in understanding the doctrine of gifts? What evidence do you have for your position?

Chapter VI

The Home As Educator

by William Hill

Introduction

When we speak metaphorically of the home as an educator, we can view the scope of Christian education from at least two perspectives. First, we may view the home from the point of view of the people involved: the husband and wife who may also be a father and a mother. Second, we can look at the home as an institution established by God. Regardless of the perspective we take on the home, we are—as Christians—agreed that the church cannot accomplish the task of Christian education alone. This is not to minimize the important contributions the church makes in the spiritual development of multitudes of people. We are only suggesting that no one institution, like no one person, can do all that needs to be done in the area of Christian education. Certainly the family needs the assistance of the Sunday school and the corporate worship with others, but, the task is too complex to be achieved in these brief periods of time we spend in our educational and church facilities.

Therefore, the home must accept willingly and intelligently its responsibility for the Christian education of children. The Bible definitely lays this burden at the feet of the parents and particularly the father. Early in the life of the Jewish people, God made this clear:

And these words, which I command thee this day, shall be in thine heart: And thou shalt teach them diligently unto thy children, and shalt talk of them when thou sittest in thine house, and when thou walkest by the way, and when thou liest down, and when thou risest up (Deuteronomy 6:6-7).

The Significance of the Home

It is our responsibility as church leaders to recognize our limitations for the totality of Christian education and to lead parents to accept their share of responsibility. This may mean that as church leaders we will need to incorporate into our program training sessions for parents in, among other things, family worship and Bible study. It is not a question of whether parents can teach religion to their children, rather it is a question of what type of religion and how well they will do so. For in the normal course of life parents pass on to their children their religious beliefs and practices. Solomon wisely states, "Train up a child in the way he should go: and when he is old, he will not depart from it" (Proverbs 22:6). Solomon was laying the responsibility at the feet of parents. Many parents do not feel qualified to teach their children in religious matters and wish to lay the task at the feet of the Sunday school teacher or the pastor. But, as we have already seen, Deuteronomy 6:6, 7 shows us that parents are to teach the Word of God to their children literally and by example in daily living. So even if we feel unqualified as parent-teachers, we cannot escape our God-given responsibilities. We must become qualified to fulfill the ministries God has given to us as parents.

Our preparation to teach our children is crucial; for, the

home lays the foundation for ideals, habits, attitudes, and religious beliefs. These things are absorbed by children almost as readily as the atmosphere they breathe. Their values are caught rather than taught. The atmosphere of the home is said to depend on the attitude of the parents toward each other, toward the child and toward God. The responsibility rests upon the parents to model these values, attitudes, behavior, and beliefs in their daily living.

In a recent study of the conversion experiences of college freshmen, some interesting information surfaced.[1] One of the questions examined in the study dealt with the age of conversion. This question was cross-tabulated with a question which asked the place of conversion. The findings revealed a higher percentage of those who reported a conversion experience between the ages of four and nine stated that the experience took place in the home. The findings of this study coincide with other research done in the field of conversion. For example, previous research has indicated that approximately 70 percent of those who come to Christ are influenced more by their parents than the Sunday school, worship services, or revival meetings.[2] From these findings, we see the greatest influence on young children is exercised by parents.

In order for parents to have this positive influence on their children, they must be both competent and consistent Christians in word and deed. The lives and teachings of parents should harmonize so that the reality of the spoken word is reflected in their daily experiences before their children. Good or bad, parents are models to their children.

An example of a negative influence is illustrated by an article appearing in Ann Landers' column several years ago. A freshman in college who had been caught cheating on a final exam was expelled. He had bought the answers for the examination for ten dollars from an upperclassman. When he arrived home his father, mother, aunt, and uncle were shocked, embarrassed, disgraced, and deeply hurt. How could he do this to such a fine upright family? When asked why, he replied, "Everybody does it."

The statement, "It's OK, kid, everybody does it!" was something he had heard all his life from significant adults in his life. When he was a young boy his father was stopped by a policeman for speeding. His father slipped the policeman a five dollar bill and evaded a speeding ticket. As they drove away his father remarked, "Everybody does it." One night when the young man was a boy, he overheard his father and uncle talking about several ways they could cheat the government on their income tax returns. After all, "Everybody does it," he heard them say. He also recalled the time he broke his glasses. His aunt came to his rescue and after some persuasion she took matters into her own hands. She called the insurance company and convinced them the boy had lost his glasses and collected twenty-seven dollars to buy a new pair. Here again the rationalization was, "Everybody does it."

Why did this young man do such a dishonorable thing? He was simply imitating his models. Children, then, naturally internalize their parents' value system, beliefs, and life style and carry these over into their adult lives. The old adage, "He's a chip off the old block," is often a reality. So often is it a reality, we are inclined to see why the Scriptures put so much emphasis on selecting pastors and deacons who have properly reared their children.

The Principle of Modeling

Modeling is so natural and so important that Paul used the principle in his relationships with his converts, calling on them to imitate him as he sought to imitate Christ. He said in his letter to the church at Corinth, that while they might have many instructors in Christ, they would still have him as their father. "Wherefore," he concluded, "I beseech you, be ye followers of me" (1 Corinthians 4:16).

Paul here is linking words, life, and spiritual power together as the model to be imitated. Parents should model the Christian life before their children. The basic issues of life are learned through identification with parents (such issues as, how parents react to stressful situations, how they relate to one another, their attitudes toward God, the Bible, sin, their neighbors, and the church). Parents and children must be involved together in building the body of Christ in the home and living out Christ's life in the world. It is, after all, what we are, not what we say, that will affect our children the most. A parent must be committed totally to Christ daily in order to have a positive Christian influence. Likewise, there must be a commitment to keep on growing, maturing, being perfected if our influence is to remain positive.

There seems to be a definite correlation between a child's concept of God and his perception of and relationship to his parents, especially to his father. Some psychologists contend that up to the age of three years in the child's life, the parents fill the place of God. In counseling young people with a "God problem" (i.e., negative views of God, doubts of his love and forgiveness), inquiry into their family relationships is frequently enlightening. In almost every situation, there is a definite problem with familial relationships, such as an absent father, punitive, unloving, unforgiving parents or a legalistic approach to Christianity.

It has been shown that if a child views his parents as judgmental, cruel, hard, unforgiving, and unloving, he may view God in a similar manner. To speak of God as Father to such a child may create fear, anger, and rebellion. On the other hand, a child who lives in a warm, loving home with stable, understanding, forgiving, secure parents is more likely to have a positive view of God and a more wholesome relationship with Him, as well as a desire to know and obey Him. Unfortunately, many parents have never outgrown their childish ideas about God, and they pass these on to their children. If for no other reason, then, we ought to seek to be Bible-believing and practicing Christians so that our children will not grow up with childish ideas about God—if indeed, they accept Him at all.

We are well aware of the fact that young people have been disillusioned by hypocrisy in political and church leaders. The greater damage is done when children recognize hypocrisy in their parents. If parents do not grow in their relationship to Christ, they will never lead their children beyond their own infantile faith. Children and parents need absolutes upon which to build stable lives. These are found in a mature faith based upon an unshakable faith in the Biblical principles.

Children also need the security of a loving parental discipline. Discipline is positive and healthy when done in love. Today there seems to be a shift away from youth's responsiveness to authority. Much of this rebellion may be youth's struggle toward independence. Parents need to exercise patience during this period and recognize that youth's struggle for independence is not always bad. Young people need to come into their own personhood and learn to think for themselves and make their own decisions in the light of what they discover in the Scriptures. Often this period of so-called rebellion is no more than an effort on the part of the young person to internalize his own faith and value system. He is seeking to own these as his personal faith and values rather than living on his parents' or church's faith.

In connection with this concept, it is important to recognize that there is a difference between authority and authoritarianism. The first, authority, is a position, and the second, authoritarianism, is a personality characteristic. Authoritarianism reflects itself in the personality that is dogmatic, cold, coercive, dictatorial. An authoritarian person demands perfection from others and punishes those who do not meet his standards. He demands loyalty and obedience and uses people to further his own programs. Most people plagued with an authoritarian complex are insecure in their own personhood and position and fear losing control. Parents may become defensive and feel threatened when their children question their beliefs. This may cause the parents to slip into the trap of authoritarianism, and rather than gaining control—using their God-given authority—they may drive their children away from themselves as well as God. This problem seems to have been upon Paul's mind when he wrote the Ephesian believers (6:4). In our own language, he was saying, "Fathers, do not be overly corrective and exasperate your children. Instead, bring them up in a manner that will be conducive to their appreciating Christian discipline and truth."

It may be that much of youth's rebellion toward God and the church may be an indirect rebellion against authoritarian parents. What better way, they may feel, to strike back at and hurt parents than to turn away from their parents' God, church, beliefs, and values. On the other hand, a position of authority is gained by the quality of one's life as a Christian. It has to be earned by one's living example. This point was stressed by Peter when he wrote that pastors are to be leaders as a result of being Christian models or examples, not as a result of setting themselves up as gods over a group of believers (1 Peter 5:3).

Perhaps one reason some children do not respect their parents is that the parents are not respectable. Children need and even want discipline, for they find security in parents who care enough to confront them in their disobedience. Permissiveness is an indication to children that parents do not care greatly for them. Discipline should be done in love, forgiveness, acceptance, and restoration; for, the major purpose for discipline is to restore the child to a loving relationship with his parents and God. Discipline is not, as some seem to think, a means of getting even with children.

In Romans 13:1-4, Paul talks about those in leadership roles in government, but the principle involved can be applied to those in leadership in the church and the home. He points out that a person in a position of authority is a servant to God and people. In a similar way, parents are servants to God and their children. Their life is concerned with taking care of and supplying the children's needs. They are to use their authority in love, not seeing their children as unnecessary interruptions of their lives.

In order to effectively teach our children Christian principles, values, and behavior we must be competent Christian examples or models before them. This observation is foundational to seeing the home as an educator, for young people want to know and grow close to adults whom they can respect as maturing Christians.

The Principle of Consistency

Not only must parents be competent Christians, but they must also reflect this competency in a daily walk with the Lord. Children need to see that the lives of their parents are consistent with the teachings of the Bible. It is very confusing for a child to hear his parents teach some Biblical truth and fail to see them live out this truth in normal daily living. As we have noted earlier, our communications by our actions and attitudes are more effective and lasting than our spoken word.

Most children like to go to Sunday school and Vacation Bible School and to learn choruses and Bible stories. One chorus that most children learn to sing is:

> Jesus loves the little children
>   All the children of the world.
> Red and yellow, black and white
>   They are precious in his sight.
> Jesus loves the little children of the world.

It must be confusing for a child to learn this chorus as a truth and then hear his Christian parents bitterly and caustically discuss minority groups. How can one, especially a child, reconcile the story of the Good Samaritan with racial prejudice? The inconsistency on the part of parents with these Biblical accounts may cause a child to either disbelieve the Bible as infallible or disbelieve the parents' Christian commitment.

How confusing it must be for a child to hear a Sunday school lesson or a sermon on love for God and each other and fail to see love expressed in the home. How does he feel when he hears his parents criticize and ridicule the neighbors when he has been taught to love his neighbor as he loves himself? How can he reconcile the Biblical teaching of joy and peace in the heart of the Christian when his home is a constant battle ground? Happy homes are not accidents. It takes time, love, understanding, patience, planning, and continuous work to build a happy contented home. Yet, God intends that a warm loving home be the best incubator and cultivator of Christian lives.

When we have a warm, loving Christian home, we will stand out in the community. Others may desire to know how this family came to achieve such life together. This may be an open door to family evangelism in the community. An effective way to do family evangelism is to invite a non-Christian family home for dinner or for an evening and live out the Christian life before them. Allow them to see the unity, love, joy, peace; but we must still be real people. We dare not wear masks or put on a false showing; for, they will see through the facade. If our Christian lives are real, they will see, desire, and inquire about the difference they see. If our Christian lives are consistent in our neighborhoods, we will have some success when we invite our neighbors to go to Sunday school and church with us.

Since both the father and the mother are responsible for the religious training of the child, they should encourage one another, challenge one another, and cultivate each other's gifts for personal growth in spiritual maturity. This may be done by praying together, sharing concerns and problems, and studying the Bible together. Husband and wife are not to compete with one another but to complement each other's strengths and weaknesses.

When the child is small, the mother is with him more than the father; therefore, she would have the greater influence. Still it is the father's responsibility as head of the home to encourage the mother and help her to be a most effective witness to the child. He may do this by studying the Bible with her, praying with her, and encouraging her to spend as much time as possible with the children in spiritual things. When the father is at home, he should take the lead in family devotions and prayer. This is especially necessary when children are small. They will develop the habit of Bible study and prayer, and when they are older they will be more likely to continue the practice on their own.

The father must also make his time with the children meaningful by playing with them, showing interest in their activities, and answering their questions. A father who is willing to give his time to his children will find a greater willingness on their part to participate in family devotions. A child is impressed and greatly influenced when he sees his father reading the Bible and praying to his Heavenly Father. A child will seek very early to imitate his parents, and since he is by nature religious, he will learn early in life to worship, pray, and live as his parents live before him.

The Question of Method

There are differences of opinion as to the most effective method of training among Christian educators. Some feel that the old-fashioned family altar has been tried and proven to be the most effective method. Scores of "how to" books have been written for family devotions, family Bible study, and Scripture memorization; therefore, we will not go into detail in this area.

When some folk think of Christian education in the home, they immediately conjure up in their minds the stereotype

image of a family seated at the supper table or in front of the
fireplace and the father reading from the large family Bible.
Then it is prayer time and off to bed. Father feels good that he
has fulfilled his Christian duty. One danger in hurrying through
a devotional time is that children may feel it is less important
than other areas of life. If the only time God is mentioned is in
praying over a meal or just before bedtime, the children may
dissect their lives into the sacred and the secular. If the sacred is
given only a couple of minutes each day they may conclude
that it is not too important to their total life.

Another danger in hurrying through a devotional time is
that children may have questions about God, the devil, Heaven,
Hell, and what it means to be saved. A parent cannot
adequately teach his child until he is aware of how much the
child understands. Family devotions can become boresome,
arduous tasks if only done out of obligation. If the children do
not participate, it is not family devotions at all, but a father or
mother simply going through the motions to ease their
consciences. Many people still feel that this is the only valid
method of Christian education in the home.

There are others who feel that important as this time is it
is not the whole of Christian education in the home. We can
never be satisfied with mere mental mastery of God's Word,
important as it is. Teaching is far more than sharing information
about a particular subject. The Bible is not only a book to be
studied, memorized, and learned, but it is a book to be lived
and experienced. The goal of our teaching must be that our
children will grow in the ability to live God's Word in a godless
world. It is experiencing God's truth that makes living God's
truth meaningful.

God is more concerned that we should experience His love

overflowing in our lives than that we should be able to theologically explain it. It is often easier to theorize than it is to actualize. It is possible to talk about faith and at the same time have little or no capacity to express that faith through life in the world. It is more important for us to see attitudes and values expressed in life than to merely rigidly follow the rules.

The conclusion of some educators is that telling is not necessarily teaching nor is listening necessarily learning. For learning takes place in the normal experiences or everyday living. This being true, parents can take advantage of daily experiences to teach the Bible in a meaningful way to their children. The Bible may be looked upon by children as an interesting book of stories of yesterday and not seen or experienced as reality. "I've heard those stories before," say the children who do not view the Bible as something relevant to today's living experiences. The Bible becomes reality when parents and children are involved together in its study, and it is viewed as God speaking to them today. In linking Bible learning to life, parents need to invite their children to share and talk over what these truths mean to them, and how they apply to their daily lives. Thus the children are involved in thinking about life: talking over feelings, experiences, choices, and values. In this way the parents get insight into the areas the children are concerned about, the questions they pose and the things they do not understand about the Bible, life, suffering, death, and eternity. Jesus was a great teacher who wove His stories around the life situations of His hearers. Parents must know where their children are in order to adequately teach them. By listening to the child, the parents may learn of the child's perspective of God. If his concepts are confused, parents may be able to correct them.

One reason some parents may prefer the family devotion method of Christian education is that it is not as demanding as creative Bible study or as difficult as the experience of daily applying Biblical truth to our lives. For instance, children often ask Biblical questions that theologians have struggled with for centuries, such as, "What does God look like?" "What is God doing now?" "Where is Hell?" "Why is there evil in the world?" Often parents give glib answers to such serious questions or simply turn the child off by ignoring the question. A parent might say to the child, "I don't know the answer. Let's talk about it and look together in the Bible or ask the pastor and see if we can find the answer." The very honesty of the parent and the concern shown can create a warm, loving relationship that will encourage the child to feel free to discuss his problems, needs, and concerns with his parents.

Almost hourly in the child's life there are opportunities to teach Biblical truths in experiences that make the content of the Bible more meaningful. By being alert and sensitive to a child's questions and daily experiences and using situations to creatively teach the Bible, the Bible may become more relevant to the parents as well as meaningful to the child. Deuteronomy 6:6, 7 seems to be teaching this truth. The fathers are commanded to have God's words in their heart and to teach them to their sons in daily life situations beginning each morning when they arise, as they sit to eat, as they walk and go about their daily tasks, and before they retire in the evening. In this way the Word of God becomes as much a part of the person's life as the very air he breathes. He can apply the teachings of Scripture to every area of his life.

This Scripture reference, Deuteronomy 6:6, 7, seems to be teaching a combination of both the direct method (Bible study, devotions, Scripture memorization) and the indirect method (daily life experiences). One method should not be used to the exclusion of the other; and we must remember that a knowledge of Bible content is necessary. As Paul said, "Study to shew thyself approved unto God, a workman that needeth not to be ashamed, rightly dividing the word of truth" (2 Timothy 2:15). But before Paul, the Psalmist exclaimed, "Thy word have I hid in mine heart, that I might not sin against thee" (Psalm 119:11).

Parents need to impress upon their children by their own example the importance of studying the Bible and knowing its content, for it is the Word of God. When children notice parents daily reading the Bible, they will seek to imitate them. Most children treasure their own Bible and proudly carry it to church.

Studying the Bible simply for head knowledge is not enough, though. Parents must teach their children how to take the great principles of Scriptures and apply them to daily living situations. It is one thing to talk about God, creation, prayer, forgiveness, love, eternal life, but it takes time and creativity to make these truths applicable in the child's daily life. The Bible, when applied to life's situations, makes the Bible come alive.

While our discussion is not designed as a "how to do it" manual, perhaps the following life situations may serve as a springboard for other creative Bible study ideas.

It is not too difficult to teach children stories from the Bible, for they are simple and direct and children can identify with them. One difficulty is making the stories real, for children often confuse Biblical stories with fairy tales they are taught. Parents must emphasize that these stories are real life stories of real people and situations that are told to teach us how to live in relationship to God, to our family, and to our neighbors.

The most difficult task is to teach children intangible but very important truths such as love, forgiveness, unselfishness, obedience, and faith. The most effective way to teach these truths is through daily life situations. It is one thing to teach a child the Ten Commandments, but it is more important to help him live out these commandments in his daily life.

Let us illustrate this point. A young boy was playing ball near his home when his mother called him to help her take a basket of food to a poor family. He replied, "Can't the maid do it mother?" "No," said his mother, "I want you to grow up to have a tender, loving, sharing heart like Jesus did. God teaches us to love our neighbor as ourself." He went along with her not just this time but many other times as well. He became a missionary to China. His mother's daily teaching had made him unselfish and loving toward others, and he expressed these qualities in his adult life.

Rather than just reading the Genesis account of creation to a child it is more effective to take him out of doors and view nature firsthand. Let him see the beauty of God's handiwork in a rose, the grass, the trees, animal life. In this setting, he will readily understand why God called His creation "good." Explain to him that God is our Heavenly Father and made all of this for us to enjoy just as his earthly father works to give him food, clothing, shelter, and toys for his enjoyment.

Many children are confused about death and eternity and often these are just words. They have a pet that dies, or a friend or relative, and they ask many questions. A father explained it to his child thus, "Son, you remember when we went to visit Grandma and Grandpa last summer? You fell asleep in the car and were still asleep when we arrived. We didn't wake you up but took you upstairs to the bedroom and tucked you in bed. The next morning when you awoke you were a little confused as you looked up at a strange ceiling and around at strange furniture. But all at once you realized you were at Grandma and Grandpa's house and you bounded out of bed and downstairs and into the arms of your grandparents. Well, son, death is something like that. We fall asleep here and wake up in Heaven with God."

Teaching a child how to pray is very important, too. He must grow out of the "Now I lay me down to sleep prayer" to a more personal communication with God. He will listen carefully to his parents' prayers and learn from them. A parent might explain to the child that praying is talking to God just like the child talks to his parents. In praying he can thank God for his food, his friends, and his home. He can also tell God when he is afraid, for the Heavenly Father is just as close and concerned as his earthly father.

Jesus taught His disciples how to pray by giving them a model prayer to go by. He did not intend for us to make this our only prayer but see it as an example of what to include in our prayers. His greatest lesson on prayer was His own living example. For the child, the greatest lesson on prayer will be his parents' prayer life.

Teaching by life situations often is more difficult and time consuming, but it is also the most effective tool for lessons that will never be forgotten. A combination of both Biblical content and real life situations can give a child a meaningful Christian education, an education that will lead to his salvation and growth in the Lord Jesus Christ.

Regardless of the method parents use to teach their children Biblical truths, they must remember that a child learns from their example. The most important aspect is in their relationship to one another and to God. If a father is too busy to be with his wife, child, or his God, his child will imitate him.

In order for Christian education to be accomplished in the home there must be a stable relationship between parent and God, and parent and child. It is doubtful that a parent can lead his child to God if there is not a meaningful, stable relationship between parent and child. Relationships are not built on separation; therefore, parents must make time for their children and this time together must be meaningful.

Conclusion

Let us briefly summarize what we have concluded in our analysis of the home as an educator. First of all, we have observed the significance of the home in the lives of children. This significance is at least twofold. The Scriptures make it abundantly clear that the home is foundational to Christian education. No church agency or educational institution, regardless of how effective it is, relieves parents of their responsibility in this realm. Also, research reflects the notion that the home is more influential for Christ than any other avenue for Christian education.

Secondly, we have seen that our example as parents either directs our children to Christ or away from Him. Likewise, we learned that the extent to which our children reflect the beauty of Christ is largely determined by the beauty of Him which they see in us.

Thirdly, the consistency with which Christ is seen in the lives of mothers and fathers is inseparably related to the attractiveness they and Christ will have to their children. Maturity in Christ, therefore, is necessary in the parents if they are to have a strong positive influence for Him.

Last of all, we pointed out the question of methodology in the home is not an either-or issue. To be effective as Christian educators, parents need to use a variety of means for reaching their children for Christ. Similarly, parents need to continue utilizing various methods to develop their faith, nurture their love, cultivate Christian virtues—to manifest the fruit of the Spirit among God's people, the church, and among the world which so desperately needs the witness of those who are enjoying eternal life in Christ.

Discussion Questions

1. According to the author, why do most homes fail to lead children to Christ and to maturity in Him? Do you agree?
2. In thinking back through your own conversion and growth in Christ, what experiences and people were most influential? Identify precisely what happened that was of greatest influence.
3. The author says that when the father is home he should lead in family devotions. Should a father be away from home very much in the light of 1 Corinthians 7:5, 33? That is, is a husband really seeking to serve ("please") his wife and to be a mate if he is away from home a great deal of the time?
4. What significant differences from the traditional, direct approach (family devotions, Bible study) would you anticipate finding if you were to observe a family which stressed the indirect approach (daily life experiences) to Christian

education in the home? What are the advantages and disadvantages of each approach?

5. The author says, "Almost hourly in the child's life there are opportunities to teach Biblical truths in experiences that make the content of the Bible more meaningful." If parents wish to take advantage of these hourly opportunities, what implications does this idea have for parent-child relationships?

6. If a Christian family matures in the Lord, the author suggests it will have the possibility of being an evangelistic instrument in the neighborhood. What methods of evangelism, other than that mentioned by the author, are also practical for the average family?

7. The author discusses the concepts of *authority* and *authoritarianism*. Do you think he clearly distinguishes between the two ideas? Do you find his discussion sound? Would you agree or disagree with his thoughts?

Chapter VII

The Pastoral Ministry

by Floyd Wolfenbarger

Introduction

Like the ministry of the family, God has specifically ordained the ministry of the pastor. The ministry of the pastor, however, has frequently been conceived of in two opposing manners. It seems there is an almost unavoidable compulsion to attach a neat label to a pastor for future reference. If we have learned the skill of marking and categorizing preachers, it is apparent that only two labels are allowable: a man is either a preacher or a teacher. A preacher has the ability to preach with "power" (*e.g.*, loudly) and "unction" *(e.g.*, breathlessly).

The teacher, on the other hand, is typically identified as having a presentation that is too neat to be powerful. He is invariably a monotone by our standards, often making reference to Bible verses, then reading them. He will put an entire congregation to sleep if it has not determined to endure hardness and remain wide-eyed to the end. In short, the minister whom we label as a teacher is a bore.

In reality the designation of preacher or teacher to either of these types is misplaced, because the style has little to do with any difference which might exist between teaching and preaching. Yet, this categorization is so fixed in many people's minds that there has arisen an unbiblical dichotomy between preaching and teaching until Christian education is viewed as a separate task altogether from the pastoral function of the minister. Biblically, Christian education is the specific domain of the pastor. If the pastor is not apt to teach, he is unqualified for his calling. If we look at the pastor from the Biblical perspective, we will see that preaching which is not teaching too is not preaching either. In examining the pastoral ministry, then, we will be avoiding this non-Biblical dichotomy.

The Pastor and His World

Several metaphors have been used to describe the relationship between the pastor and the world in which he is planted. Some suggest that the pastor's relationship to the world should be one of separation, nothing else. Others contend that he should identify himself with the world. The Biblical metaphors and titles of the pastor give a clearer insight into the pastor's relationship to the world.

First, the pastor must be an evangelist to the world, to that part of the world where God has placed him, to his specific world. Paul charges Timothy to "do the work of an evangelist" (2 Timothy 4:5). Paul's instruction did not mean that Timothy should have left the pastoral ministry and held evangelistic crusades in various cities of Asia Minor. Paul apparently viewed evangelism as an important focus for the pastoral ministry not something entirely separate. Evangelism is the process of making clear to unbelievers that the will of God for them is repentance of sins and trusting in the Lord Jesus Christ. It is *teaching* the uninformed and unregenerate of God's redemptive plan, using the most understandable language to convey this thought to them.

This is clearly the initial stage of Christian education.

There is no dichotomy, therefore, between teaching and evangelism. The pastor is called upon as an evangelist to teach persuasively the basic truths of the gospel message. The unregenerate mind cannot discern or welcome the various types of theology that are in circulation today; therefore, the unbeliever must be taught of his need for God and God's love for him.

Second, the pastor must be an ambassador in his relationship to his particular world. Paul writes to the Ephesians reminding them that their warfare is not with the "flesh and blood" people who live in the world. Their conflict is with Satan, the prince of power of the air, who empowers the children of disobedience. If our warfare today is not with people who are directed by Satan, what is our relationship with the sinner? We are ambassadors. The Christian pastor is an ambassador who is commissioned to reconcile non-Christians to Christ, declare His ultimate victory, and to lead an exemplary life which becomes his heavenly citizenship. This ambassadorial metaphor emphasizes the teaching role of the pastor, who communicates God's desire to make peace with the sinner.

An ambassador also is called upon to negotiate marriages. The pastor, in keeping with the mataphor, is called upon to invite the unregenerate to turn to Christ as a bride would desire a bridegroom. He offers to the unregenerate gifts of His unsearchable riches as a seal of His wedding commitment.

Furthermore, an ambassador is viewed as a representative of his country. If an ambassador is perceived as a greedy knave, then it will be assumed that his government is likewise corrupt. A minister teaches not only by proclamation and formal preaching, but also by his decorum. Many ministers who have been bitter and churlish men have unjustly betrayed a compassionate church and a merciful King. In so doing, they have disgraced their Master before the world. Ambassadors are teachers not only by what they say, but especially by what they are.

The Pastor and His Church

In addition to the pastor having the responsibility of being an educator to the uninformed and unsaved about the elementary principles of God's judgment and grace, he also has a particular responsibility to a specific congregation of believers which we call the church. In some respects the pastor may be viewed as distinct from the church as a whole; however, he is also a part of the church. He is both a shepherd and a sheep, a teacher and a student, a builder and a brick. He can never escape from the implications of his own teachings; for he, too, is a part of the congregation to whom he is declaring divine truth. As a pastor of a church, we may see him from several angles.

First, we may see the pastor as a parent. This important comparison is found in the writings of Paul to the Thessalonians. The following lengthy quotation beautifully conveys this thought:

> But as we were allowed of God to be put in trust
> with the gospel, even so we speak; not as pleasing
> men, but God, which trieth our hearts. For neither at
> any time used we flattering words, as ye know, nor a
> cloke of covetousness; God is witness: Nor of men

sought we glory, neither of you, nor yet of others, when we might have been burdensome, as the apostles of Christ. But we were gentle among you, even as a nurse cherisheth her children: So being affectionately desirous of you, we were willing to have imparted unto you, not the gospel of God only, but also our own souls, because ye were dear unto us. For ye remember, brethern, our labour and travail: for labouring night and day, because we would not be chargeable unto any of you, we preached unto you the gospel of God. Ye are witnesses, and God also, how holily and justly and unblameably we behaved ourselves among you that believe: As ye know how we exhorted and comforted and charged every one of you, as a father doth his children, That ye would walk worthy of God, who hath called you unto his kingdom and glory (1 Thessalonians 2:4-12).

This lovely passage points to the training given new converts (the Thessalonians had been converted only a few months prior to this writing) by Paul who compared himself to a nurse/mother who gently feeds a child and the father who teaches his children to walk. An Old Testament proverb often referred to in Christian educational literature draws a similar picture. "Train up a child in the way he should go: and when he is old, he will not depart from it" (Proverbs 22:6). The Hebrew word *chanak* ("train up") means "to put to the mouth, to offer to taste." The image is of a nurse/mother who first masticates food to be given an infant. The Christian pastor, like such a nurse, tastes of God's holiness and imparts its richness to the babe in Christ. Paul said to note that he had not only fed them the gospel but that this gospel had already been processed in his own experience. It was as though he gave them both Christ and his own soul.

It seems clear that the responsibilities given to the pastor in the education of new converts are great. These responsibilities transcend the preaching ministry in a formal setting and extend to the giving of oneself to the family of Christ. This giving relationship is without guarantee of return; for even Paul feared that his giving of himself to the Thessalonians might have been in vain (1 Thessalonians 3:5). Nonetheless, he went on giving, for that is the genuine meat of teaching. Nor was this devotion of a parent/teacher limited to new converts. For on another occasion, Paul reiterated this truth when he wrote the Corinthian believers:

> Behold, the third time I am ready to come to you; and I will not be burdensome to you: for I seek not yours, but you: for the children ought not to lay up for the parents, but the parents for the children. And I will very gladly spend and be spent for you; though the more abundantly I love you, the less I be loved . . . . Again, think ye that we excuse ourselves unto you? we speak before God in Christ: but we do all things, dearly beloved, for your edifying (2 Corinthians 12:14, 15, 19).

The Christian pastor teaches from a parental relationship, one that gives without the necessity of receiving. He teaches, not for its remuneration, but for the joy of seeing his spiritual children grow and be edified or built up into a spiritual family. The pastoral ministry is much more than a contracted program of teaching and administration. It is not a job to be done, but a responsibility. This parental relationship separates the genuine pastor from the hired teacher.

Second, the Christian pastor is a farmer. Pastors have often been compared to those who cultivate the ground, sow the seed, prune the vine, guard the fruit, and reap the harvest. Paul uses this metaphor in a fluent discussion of the way diversity among ministers is unified by God's use of their ministries:

> Who then is Paul, and who is Apollos, but ministers by whom ye believed, even as the Lord gave to every man? I have planted, Apollos watered; but God gave the increase. So then neither is he that planteth any thing, neither he that watereth; but God that giveth the increase. Now he that planteth and he that watereth are one.... For we are laborers together with God (1 Corinthians 3:5-9).

This passage indicates that the labor of the pastor as he teaches does not yield immediate fruit. The pastor may proclaim a divine truth again and again without being sure of its ultimate result. When seed is planted, only time will tell if the seed will grow to a fruitbearing plant. It is not always easy to teach and preach, sowing the seed, without seeing the fruit of one's labor, but the pastor must look beyond immediate fruit toward the ultimate.

Further, Paul seems to say that a pastor is not working alone. He is adding to someone else's labors. One will plant while another waters. Ministers have an important role in bringing the seed-truth to a fruitbearing plant, but they do not successfully do their work alone. This knowledge should help reduce the danger of pride. Both Paul and Apollos were nothing of themselves. The credit for the fruitful harvest belongs to God. The farmer cannot "grow" grain or beets or grapes; he can, however, endeavor to provide an atmosphere by planting, cultivating, and watering which is conducive to growth. Pride has no place in the Christian pastor who sows, waters, or reaps because he should know the increase is God's.

In addition the Christian pastor who realizes that some sow, others water, and so forth, will not easily despair in his task. He is obligated to do his best, but he is not responsible for doing everything. Some pastors have been very fortunate to be leaders of excellent churches whose former pastors had left behind an excellent core of workers who were the product of those pastors' ministries. These fortunate pastors should strive to continue training Christians who will assist even later pastors. While no minister is obliged to teach everything to everyone, everywhere, he ought to add his gift to the growth which was initiated by others. So then, Paul concluded that he and Apollos were laborers together with God though they labored at different times and in different ways.

Finally, the Christian pastor is a shepherd. This metaphor is intrinsic in the term itself. The word *pastor* in the King James Version is found only once in the New Testament. The word appears in Paul's epistle to the Ephesian believers:

> And he gave some, apostles; and some, prophets;
> and some, evangelists; and some, pastors and teachers;
> For the perfecting of the saints, for the work of the
> ministry, for the edifying of the body of Christ: Till
> we all come in the unity of the faith, and of the
> knowledge of the Son of God, unto a perfect man,
> unto the measure of the stature of the fulness of

Christ: That we henceforth be no more children, tossed to and fro, and carried about with every wind of doctrine, by the sleight of men, and cunning craftiness, whereby they lie in wait to deceive; But speaking the truth in love, may grow up into him in all things, which is the head, even Christ: From whom the whole body fitly joined together and compacted by that which every joint supplieth, according to the effectual working in the measure of every part, maketh increase of the body unto the edifying of itself in love (Ephesians 4:11-16).

The Greek word *poimēn* which is rendered "pastor" in this passage is translated "shepherd" the other seventeen times it is used in the New Testament. The emphasis of the word is that of a "feeder-man."

The teaching dynamic of the shepherd has a different emphasis from the imagery of the nurse/mother. The shepherd does not prepare a meal and dose it out to the sheep. Instead, the shepherd guides the flock from one green valley to another. In like manner the Christian pastor guides his flock as he leads them through the green pastures of God's Word. He does this unendingly. The role of the pastor in Christian education is like a shepherd in that no Christian education is ever complete. At no point is the task ever finished until the Chief Shepherd shall bring His reward.

Furthermore, the methods of the shepherd are worth observing. He cares for the sheep by feeding them, watching them, and leading them. Peter's admonition to pastors makes this clear. His own words are as follows:

The elders which are among you I exhort, who

am also an elder, and a witness of the sufferings of Christ, and also a partaker of the glory that shall be revealed: Feed the flock of God which is among you, taking the oversight thereof, not by constraint, but willingly; not for filthy lucre, but of a ready mind; Neither as being lords over God's heritage, but being ensamples to the flock. And when the chief Shepherd shall appear, ye shall receive a crown of glory that fadeth not away (1 Peter 5:1-4).

This threefold methodology—feeding, watching, and leading—should be more often utilized. The methodology of feeding has already been pointed out; the shepherd also must keep a vigilant watch over the sheep. This means that pastors teach by protection, ever watching for the pitfalls hewn out by Satan, the adversary of men's souls. A watchful shepherd is concerned about numbers; ninety-nine is not enough if one hundred are in the fold. He is to be intimately attached to the flock. Taking oversight must imply that the shepherd is there with the sheep. Far too many flocks today are left unattended by overly ambitious shepherds who spend too much time feeding other flocks. A shepherd cares for his sheep not only by the proclamations he makes but also by the encouragement of his presence.

The final methodology of the shepherd described by Peter is leading. Some translators have translated *poimēn* "guide." It is certainly a worthy emphasis. The shepherd leads the sheep along a safe path. He goes before them and they follow after. This demonstrates the courage of the shepherd. The Christian pastor must lead by example. Paul invited men to follow him as he was following Christ. This matter of teaching by example should pervade the whole personality. Doctrines which the pastor experiences he will also teach. Paul candidly addresses Timothy on this question:

> Let no man despise thy youth; but be thou an example of the believers, in word, in conversation, in charity, in spirit, in faith, in purity. Till I come, give attendance to reading, to exhortation, to doctrine. Neglect not the gift that is in thee, which was given thee by prophecy, with the laying on of the hands of the presbytery. Meditate upon these things; give thyself wholly to them; that thy profiting may appear to all. Take heed unto thyself, and unto the doctrine; continue in them: for in doing this thou shalt both save thyself, and them that hear thee (1 Timothy 4:12-16).

In this address to Timothy, Paul is suggesting that the welfare of the flock is as dependent upon the example set by its pastor as it is upon the doctrines he proclaims.

The admonition to lead by example is accompanied by a warning from Peter that the flock belongs not to the pastor but to God: It is the Lord's heritage which is entrusted to the pastor. He is a trustee or guardian. He does not have the option to scatter, divide, or slaughter the sheep. He is called upon only to feed, watch, and lead them. The pastor's attitude toward the flock is an indicator of his respect for the Chief Shepherd and His commission.

In relation to the church, the pastor is a parent, a farmer, and a shepherd. He is also a ruler, prophet, priest, builder, angel, messenger, laborer, and steward. All of these Biblical figures of speech emphasize different areas of teaching about the pastoral ministry and make a fruitful study for the eager student of the Scriptures. We must leave the topic, however, and review several areas of the pastor's ministry.

The Pastor and His Ministry

Several aspects of ministry are placed upon the responsible man of God. These areas of ministry describe the various means by which he tends, nurses, and cultivates the congregation and, thereby, fulfills his calling to the pastorate. These ways of teaching are as follows: 1) fellowship, 2) worship, 3) administration, 4) training. Each of these concepts will be examined briefly.

Fellowship may be the most effective means of Christian education although historically it has often been misunderstood by us. The concept does not refer to giving a hearty handshake after the worship service. Nor is fellowship simply an ice cream social after a service in the "fellowship hall." Conversely, fellowship is the compassionate sharing of the riches of Christ with others. It occurs when one Christian bears the burden of another. It is unity and singleness of heart of those who serve Christ together. This unity causes believers to share the hope, joy, and sorrows of the other's experience. Paul shares this in his letter to Corinth: "Not for that we have dominion over your faith, but are helpers of your joy: for by faith ye stand" (2 Corinthians 1:24).

The pastor, then, is a "helper of joy" and this joy is a great strength to a local body of Christians. The pastor's role in fellowship is not give and take but simply give. By giving of himself in fellowship to the whole body, he will benefit at the same time himself. The reason this is true is that he is a part of the fellowship. What he teaches he also learns. As the body is edified so is the pastor. As he knows the fellowship of their sufferings or their hopes, he is able to teach them.

Fellowship was also a major tool of evangelism in the early church. As we have already established, evangelism is teaching the gospel message in a simplified manner. The testimony of the fellowship of the early church is well documented in Scripture. Luke informs us of the following practice:

> And they, continuing daily with one accord in the temple, and breaking bread from house to house, did eat their meat with gladness and singleness of heart, Praising God, and having favour with all the people. And the Lord added to the church daily such as should be saved (Acts 2:46, 47).

These verses describe a condition which was ordinary in the early church. It was fellowship.

Fellowship is that kind of singleness of heart which is necessary for effective Christian prayer. In Biblical terms, fellowship is the "two agreeing, touching any one thing" which gives additional hope and confidence. No gift can be used by the pastor which will advance believers more in the fruitfulness of love, joy, peace, longsuffering, gentleness, goodness, faith, meekness, and temperance than to teach them fellowship. For the fruit of Christ's Spirit will cause men to live in harmony.

Another important means of ministering to the church is by providing means for *worship*. The word for worship originally had reference to the obedient labors of slaves and came to be used in connection with obeisance or "bowing down." It calls to mind reverential fear. Today the word is sometimes used to refer to services that are little more reverent than circus performances. There is a need to restore a sense of reverential fear in those who hear God's Word.

In the Scriptures, we find a close correlation between the elements of fearing, hearing, and learning. Worship is a teaching tool. This is appropriately and dramatically demonstrated in Deuteronomy 31:12, 13:

> Gather the people together, men, and women, and children, and thy stranger that is within thy gates, that they may hear, and that they may learn, and fear the Lord your God, and observe to do all the words of this law: And that their children, which have not known anything, may hear, and learn to fear the Lord your God, as long as ye live in the land whither ye go over Jordan to possess it.

This passage implies a formal setting in which everyone is gathered to one place. The purpose of the gathering is that people may *learn (lamad* in the Scriptures usually refers to moral learning) and *fear* God. The purpose of worship gatherings today must include the teaching of God's moral law and a reverent fear of His holiness.

The pastor, therefore, is charged with creating an atmosphere of reverence so the people will learn to fear and observe the will of the Almighty God. Few twentieth century sermons are preached which declare to people a God who is high and lofty. Yet the Scriptures inform us that even very young children "which have not known anything" may sense this majestic greatness of God.

The pastor teaches from other elements of worship in addition to preaching. Paul instructs the Colossians of the teaching power of music:

> And let the peace of God rule in your hearts, to the which also ye are called in one body; and be ye thankful. Let the word of Christ dwell in you richly in all wisdom; teaching and admonishing one another in psalms and hymns and spiritual songs, singing with grace in your hearts to the Lord. And whatsoever ye do in word or deed, do all in the name of the Lord Jesus, giving thanks to God and the Father by him (Colossians 3:15-17).

It is quite apparent that the songs used in worship have an important part in the teaching ministry of the church. The pastor should take a responsible approach to the message in the songs of worship if he is to avoid two extremes we find in our churches today. One extreme is songs sung for their rhythmic or emotional appeal alone. We may all have observed churches singing songs which contradicted their own doctrine because the tune was rhythmically stimulating. We should not naively assume that the messages of these songs have been harmless. On the other hand, some pastors have insisted on songs which are theologically sound but practically beyond the understanding of the congregation. Neither extreme in music fulfills the one criterion the Bible gives for worship songs. The songs must not only teach a truth but they must also make it understandable.

The pastor also teaches through the symbolic worship. The symbols of worship are those in the ordinances of the gospel. The teaching impact of the ordinances and their symbolism is very important. In the Old Testament, the observances of priests reminded people of their need for cleansing and God's willingness to forgive them their sin. This forgiveness was offered not unconditionally but according to God's prescribed plan. Today the same lessons are demonstrated in the holy ordinances that man's cleansing is accomplished by God's planned acceptance of His infinite sacrifice.

The pastor also teaches by *administration*. It is necessary that administrative abilities be developed in the pastoral ministry. The introduction of Sunday school into the teaching ministry of the church has opened the minds of Christian churches and pastors to an entire gamut of educational agencies. Vacation Bible School in many churches surpasses record Sunday school attendance in its daily average. Preschools, nursery schools, kindergarten, day schools, academies, institutes, and even college campuses are now being administrated by pastors in churches all over America.

The pastor whose church includes any or all of these extensions of the church's ministry is soon open to becoming frustrated. He has a great opportunity to teach practical faith as he governs building plans, new ministries, and oversees a growing organization. He must be very careful to be scrupulously honest. Many churches today are having great difficulties in financing the expansion of their ministry because a few somewhat infamous pastors have engaged in questionable practices. Such failures inevitably teach lessons not only to unbelievers but to the young in faith whose confidence is crushed.

We must also remember that people may treat others, as the pastor, by example, teaches them. Pastors must learn to encourage, motivate, direct, and lead others in a spirit of genuine forbearance, long-suffering, and meekness.

Finally, the pastor teaches by means of *training*. For the purpose of our discussion, *training* will refer to that aspect of teaching which relates to a specific task or skill. Much of the teaching of the pastor is aimed at teaching men to become more like Christ. In short, he teaches them to live the Christian life. Training, on the other hand, refers to teaching individuals how to be more effective as teachers, preachers, deacons, ushers, and so on. The most obvious charge which refers to this teaching of teachers comes again from the writings of Paul to Timothy: "Thou therefore, my son, be strong in the grace that is in Christ Jesus. And the things that thou hast heard of me among many witnesses, the same commit thou to faithful men, who shall be able to teach others also" (2 Timothy 2:1, 2).

Many pastors have young men in the church who have testified of a call to the ministry. The pastor is committed by Scripture to charge, encourage, and teach these young men so that they will be nourished up in the gospel of the Lord Jesus. If teachers are untrained, the pastor should oversee their instruction, too. Likewise, pastors are to charge deacons to do their work soberly and vigilantly.

This training might be accomplished in a formal setting such as an institute; however, it must be accomplished by open lines of communication. Then, too, we are not following the teachings of the Scripture when we completely turn over this task to institutes, colleges, and seminaries. Paul's letters to Timothy, Titus, and others indicate a less structured way of teaching those we have won to the Lord. Additionally, he is known to have often visited or been visited by his converts. It is by walking and talking with Jesus that the disciples were trained. Pastors should spend time with budding leaders; this will prove to be effective training.

Conclusion

In conclusion, it seems that everything a pastor is responsible to do has an important teaching element. If there is a difference between teaching and preaching, it relates to the setting and content which is divine truth. But the pastoral ministry is mainly a teaching ministry. It cannot be excluded from the Christian education ministry of the church. Biblically, we do not see the educational ministry on one side and the pastoral ministry on the other. The education or equipping of the saints is a pastoral responsibility.

The pastor is responsible to educate believers as well as unbelievers in the Word of Christ. God requires that all, regardless of age, sex, or nationality, learn of Him. All of us should remember that it is God who must ultimately judge the pastor's ministry. Thus, as Paul says:

> Therefore seeing we have this ministry, as we have received mercy, we faint not; But have renounced the hidden things of dishonesty, not walking in craftiness, nor handling the word of God deceitfully; but by manifestation of the truth commending ourselves to every man's conscience in the sight of God. But if our gospel be hid, it is hid to them that are lost: In whom the god of this world hath blinded the minds of them which believe not, lest the light of the glorious gospel of Christ, who is the image of God, should shine unto them. For we preach not ourselves, but Christ Jesus the Lord; and ourselves your servants for Jesus' sake (2 Corinthians 4:1-5).

Discussion Questions

1. Does the author adequately defend his idea that the "pastor is called upon as an evangelist to teach persuasively the basic truths of the gospel message"? What additional evidence can you give to support his view?
2. What do you think the author means when he says the pastor's responsibilities "transcend the preaching ministry in a formal setting and extend to the giving of oneself to the family of Christ"? Illustrate his position by giving examples.
3. In the author's discussion, he presents several metaphors including those of the shepherd and the parent. What types of Christians would most need a shepherd? a parent? Why do you think so?
4. The author claims, "Far too many flocks are left unattended by overly ambitious shepherds who spend too much time feeding other flocks." How often should pastors be away from their flocks? Why do you say so?
5. Why do you think the author believes that fellowship "may be the most effective means of Christian education"? Do you agree with him? Why?
6. What are some definite and practical ways pastors can train young men who plan to become ministers?

Chapter VIII

The Church Staff

by Paul F. Hall

Introduction

In the two previous chapters, we have noted that the Christian education ministries of parents and pastors are specifically commanded by God. The people who serve as church staff members are not exactly in the same category as parents and pastors, however. This observation is supported by the absence of discussion in the Scriptures about directors of education, music, youth, visitation, and so forth.

On the other hand, we ought not to be misled by this observation. Simply because these and other staff positions are not commanded in the Scriptures does not mean it is unwise to have such. Naturally, we do not have to have these staff members since they are not commanded, but the notion of staff members—without the special titles—is suggested in the ideas that church members are to minister to each other (Ephesians 4) and the gifts of the Spirit (1 Corinthians 12). Since we have discussed these thoughts in previous chapters, we will refrain from any emphasis on them, except an incidental emphasis. At this point, we simply wish to state our general plan for discussing the church staff. The following topics will be examined: a) the need for an expanded staff, b) the sources for an expanded staff, c) suggested staff positions and job descriptions, d) the relationships to be maintained between members of the church staff, and e) some general standards for selecting members of the church staff.

The Need for an Expanded Staff

For many years most of our churches and their ministries could be maintained through the efforts of one man, the pastor, in each congregation. Sometimes, especially in rural or sparsely populated areas, a pastor was a man who worked at a full-time secular occupation while performing his pastoral duties in his spare time. The church simply "got along" with this kind of arrangement but found it difficult to provide a concentrated thrust into the community with the message of the gospel.

Gradually our churches began seeing the need for a pastor who could devote his full time to the ministry of the local church. As people determined to adequately provide for the financial needs of the pastor, they found their ministry strengthened and their number began to grow. Because there was a man in the community who could represent the church day in and day out, and because there was a man upon whom the people could call at any hour of the day or night, the church became a stronger influence in people's lives and more and more converts were won and added to the membership.

This increased number is one of the determining factors relating to the need of an expanded church staff. In a growing church, it becomes more and more difficult for the pastor to perform all the duties expected of him and still be what he wants and should be to his family. The sheer weight of numbers drives the average pastor beyond his capacity and calls for some relief in the form of additional staff members who can carry some of the load.

Of course, the growth of numbers in the church creates a need for expanded ministries in its programs. Where once the church could be maintained and challenged through simple preaching and singing services, now we hear a call for definite areas of service and activity for the church members. Many churches are beginning to offer auxiliary services such as a day care nursery, Christian school, nursing homes for the aged, and even recreation programs for the youth. These services are in addition to the increased activities of music, Bible teaching, visitation, special interest groups, teacher training, bus ministries, and the building of facilities to house it all. We ask too much of one man, the pastor, if we ask him to supervise all these activities, be personally involved in them, and still expect him to perform well in his primary role, that of being a spiritual counselor and preacher of the Word.

The overwhelming spiritual need of every community cries out for the church to be reaching people with its message of forgiveness and hope. To be effective in our response to that need, we are forced to think in terms of additional personnel to carry that message by every means possible. It is this cry for help, more than numerical growth, that will ultimately determine whether a church actually needs to add additional personnel to its staff. A thorough analysis of that need and a projection concerning what methods and ministries will be needed to meet it will determine the function and number of additional staff for the local church. The church that does not see this need and does nothing to try to meet it will soon find itself beginning to die numerically and spiritually.

The Sources for an Expanded Staff

Two questions usually confront us in relation to the matter of an expanded church staff. They are as follows: a)

Where will we get the money to pay additional personnel? and b) Where will we find the people to fill the positions needed in our situation? These questions are important, and the answers ought to be given serious and prayerful thought.

Lack of finances should not keep our church from having a staff of people who can help carry the weight of maintaining an active ministry. Any church which has a Sunday school with a teacher in every class already has the nucleus of an expanded church staff serving in a voluntary capacity. Though they receive no salary, they serve specific functions in the program of the local church. The same sort of arrangement can be worked out for other staff positions.

This being the case, then, let us first look at the possibility of a volunteer staff. Every church has those members who have special abilities and talents—gifts of the Spirit—which should be put to use in the programs of our local churches. For instance, there is probably any number of women in the average church who work in secular jobs as typists or secretaries who would be delighted to give two or three hours of their time each week working in the church office to turn out newsletters, bulletins, and other correspondence. There might be professional teachers, already trained and certified in public instruction, who could assume the duties of administering the Christian education ministry of the church. Other talents and abilities could be found by conducting a simple survey to find what job skills were available to the church and how many would be willing to use those job skills in the service of the Lord. After conducting the survey, it might be helpful to discuss and categorize findings in terms of the gifts of the Holy Spirit (Romans 12; 1 Corinthians 12).

Care should be taken in the selection of these volunteers to serve in staff positions. Just because a person volunteers for a job does not mean he or she can be used. Steps should be taken to determine his degree of Christian dedication and commitment to Christian standards of conduct. The testimony of the church could be seriously harmed by a staff member who volunteered only to have some psychological need for authority satisfied in the church. A screening committee should be selected to approve all applicants for volunteer positions in the church. A primary function of this committee would be to determine if those who have gifts of the Spirit are also being filled by Him and are manifesting His fruit (1 Corinthians 13; Ephesians 5:18; Galatians 5:22-26).

Job descriptions should be clear and well publicized in the church in order for every volunteer to be well informed as to what is expected of him. Misunderstandings and confusion will result in our churches if volunteers are allowed to function without clear instructions concerning their jobs.

Another approach to securing staff members is by hiring them on a part-time basis. When we do not have funds to pay adequately a full-time worker in a local situation, we may have enough money available to justify a part-time staff member. Many churches pay an hourly wage for work done, especially for office and custodial work. This part-time arrangement can be a blessing for the church and a help to those who need the extra income. A homemaker whose children are in school all day makes an excellent part-time church secretary, perhaps coming to work four or five hours each day, Monday through Friday of each week. A retired minister may be an excellent candidate for a part-time assistant pastor.

Almost every position in the church staff that calls for a concentrated thrust could be filled by part-time staff members.

Musicians, ministers, clerical workers, and custodial help can all be maintained through this part-time arrangement.

Care should be taken to make certain that the wage paid is appropriate for the services rendered and that proper supervision is exercised over those who serve in this capacity. Since a salary is being paid, there can be a greater degree of accountability as it relates to individual responsibility.

Our final possibility for staff personnel is to employ full-time people. Those who would be candidates for the full-time staff of a local church should be those who have felt a special calling to give themselves fully to the work of the Lord. Usually they will have taken advantage of any formal training available to them in Christian colleges, Bible colleges, or institutes of practical training. They should be considered in the same manner as the church would consider a new pastor, and a call should be extended from the congregation.

Some Christian training institutions maintain active lists of students who are qualified in specific areas of Christian service. Contact can be made with such an institution and an interview arranged with candidates. In the interview, both the screening committee and the candidate should be open and honest in expressing their views and in describing exactly what will be expected of the staff member who fills the position under consideration.

We make a mistake when we expect our staff members to make a sacrifice in order to work with us. Any Christian worker who is not adequately compensated for his or her labor or talent may soon become dissatisfied. Although the dedicated Christian worker is usually willing to make more of a sacrifice than we should expect of him, it normally is not fair to allow him to do so. We must be willing to pay our church workers livable wages, in line with what others may be earning in similar secular jobs. If we are either unable or unwilling to treat fairly prospective staff members, it would be better that we not consider hiring them at all.

Suggested Staff Positions and Job Descriptions

The positions required in any local situation depend entirely upon the need present and the desire of each congregation to be involved in meeting the need. No staff position should ever be created or sustained simply to provide a position for someone, regardless of how talented or personally likable he is, unless that position is being utilized to perform a definite function and meet a specific need. Thus, our suggestions concerning staff positions are made only for the purpose of outlining specific responsibilities and listing jobs that are useful in maintaining the thrust of an active Christian witness in the program of the church.

Staff positions may not always be limited to single purpose job descriptions. It is possible, and even very likely, that most churches would desire to have staff members who can perform more than one function. For instance, when a screening committee is searching for a director of youth ministries, it often requires the candidate to have capabilities in the music ministry and in pastoral work. Only very large churches are able to have single purpose staff positions. The average church must require multipurpose positions that fill more than one need. For that reason the suggested staff positions mentioned would, in most cases, need to be combined or altered in order to meet the individual needs of the local church.

The following staff positions are those commonly found in active churches today. The larger the church the more of them we will find, but one or more of them will be found in almost every church. We should keep in mind that staff positions need to be viewed in terms of God's gifts to individual believers and not simply in terms of job descriptions. In an earlier chapter, we examined the gifts of the Spirit in terms of office gifts, speaking gifts, and serving gifts. The first two staff positions are definitely office gifts. From time to time, some of the others may be also. Gifts that are probably different examples of speaking gifts will be needed by those staff members who will be directors of Christian education, music, youth, bus, evangelism, and communications. The last three staff positions—secretary, business manager, and custodian—appear to be serving gifts.

First, let us look at the position of *the pastor*, an office gift. This is the highest staff position in the local church. The duties of pastors frequently include each of the ensuing: a) directing the spiritual thrust of the church program through preaching and teaching of the Scriptures, b) administering the day-to-day business affairs of the church within the authority granted by the church in regular business session, c) supervising the activities of all other staff positions, d) maintaining personal contact with the members of the congregation and the community at large through active visitation, counseling, and ministering in special situations, and e) setting an example for the congregation in his own personal dedication, purity of conduct, compassion in soul-winning, and involvement in the total program of the local church.

Our church may also have *an assistant or associate pastor*. An associate pastor is needed when a church develops to the extent that the pastor alone cannot adequately minister to its members. The associate pastor, therefore, is for the purpose of providing the additional help a church needs. Normally, the associate pastor will have the following responsibilities: a) performing duties assigned to him by the pastor, b) relieving the pastor by assuming some of the administrative duties for assigned programs within the program of the church, c) preaching in regular services when the pastor requests such.

The director of Christian education is a third staff position worthy of attention and begins our list of speaking gifts. The responsibilities generally involved in filling this position are along the following lines: a) directing the development of the Christian education ministry of the church; b) supervising the operation and personnel of the Sunday school, day school, Vacation Bible School, and other strictly educational activities of the church; c) serving as a resource person for those involved in the educational ministry; d) serving as chairman of the Committee on Christian Education in the local church program. In some situations, this position also involves the responsibility of writing the teaching materials used in the various educational ministries of the church.

The fourth position of interest to us is that of *the director of music ministries*. The nature of this office requires that the person filling it have some natural ability and training in music. The responsibilities included in this position are in the ensuing realms: a) directing and developing choirs in the church at every age level; b) giving personal instruction to individuals and small groups who perform; c) encouraging the organization of orchestras, rhythm bands, and instrumental talent among the people; and d) aiding the overall witness of the church by being personally responsible for the spiritual thrust of the music.

A *director of youth ministries*, unlike the previously mentioned staff members, is concerned with one particular age level. This position is becoming a standard staff position in large churches. In addition to a number of other characteristics, it is necessary that a youth minister have a personal rapport with the youth in the church. His responsibilities are of the sort delineated below: a) planning and supervising youth activities designed to promote spiritual growth among young people; b) counseling the youth concerning their life plans and problems; c) maintaining an active personal contact with the youth; and d) leading the youth into a personal relationship with Christ of salvation and/or commitment.

A relatively new staff position is that of the *director of bus ministries*. This staff position was created because of the recent thrust of local churches in reaching beyond their normal constituency to bring the unsaved under the sound of the gospel. Among the bus director's ministries we find the following: a) challenging and enlisting workers to be involved in the development of bus routes and in active visitation of their riders; b) maintaining an active training program for bus captains and pastors, enabling them to win their riders to Christ; c) keeping accurate records of maintenance and repair of the equipment utilized; and d) opening up new areas of work as the bus ministry expands.

Many large churches have added a seventh position, *the director of visitation evangelism*, as a part of their regular staff. The person who fills this position will ordinarily engage in such activities as follows: (a) directing the visitation program of the church; (b) challenging and encouraging people to be actively involved in a personal soul-winning ministry through training seminars and classes; (c) conducting canvasses of the community to find prospects for the Sunday school and church; (d) maintaining up-to-date records of those contacted and the results of the contact; and (e) winning people to Christ in a day-to-day program of personal witnessing.

Only the very large church can provide the need and challenge to justify the position of *director of Christian communications*. The responsibilities included for a person who has this position are the following: (a) editing and publishing all printed communications from the church to its constituency; (b) designing up-to-date promotional material for use in presenting the ministry of the church to the community at large; (c) publishing tracts, sermons, so forth, for use in reaching the unsaved, and (d) challenging others to be involved in a Christian literature ministry through training classes.

There can be no more valuable person in the program of the local church than *the church secretary* if the one filling this position has really been given a serving gift and develops into a capable and efficient worker. Generally stated, the responsibilities of the secretary are of the following type: (a) serving as personal secretary to the pastor; (b) keeping accurate membership records, including statistical information such as birth, death, baptism, offices held, and so on; (c) keeping up-to-date mailing lists for the membership; (d) serving as receptionist and channeling all communications to the proper personnel in the church staff; and (e) doing all duties normally pertaining to a secretary such as filing and typing.

Larger churches have found it efficient and orderly to have this staff position, that of *business manager or financial secretary*, responsible for the *financial* dealings of the church. The duties of the person who holds such a position include the ensuing: (a) supervising the counting of all monies and depositing the same in a local bank; (b) maintaining accurate records of income and expenses in a fashion that can be reported regularly and clearly to the church; (c) writing of all checks related to paying of bills and the payroll of the church; (d) receiving of bids and authorizing all purchases for the church program; and (e) supervising all secular and governmental business relations of the church.

Although other staff positions could be mentioned, we will stop with our discussion of *the custodian*. If the church is to be maintained well and present a physical testimony to the glory of God, this position must be filled by a conscientious, hard-working person who considers the job a calling from the Lord. Or, in terms of Paul's discussion in 1 Corinthians 12, he eagerly wants to use the gift of helps which the Holy Spirit has given to him. His duties embrace the activities mentioned herein after: (a) supervising the thorough cleaning of the entire church plant; (b) performing needed repairs within normal maintenance expectations; (c) maintaining the grounds in such a way as to present a trimmed and cared-for appearance to the community; (d) supervising the heating and cooling of the building when being utilized for worship services and other gatherings; and (e) seeing that the building is open and ready for all regular services by being unlocked, cleaned, and either heated or cooled depending upon the season.

In a sense, there are as many staff positions as there are needs to be met in the program of the local church. Or we can look at it this way: There are as many staff positions as there are gifted people. We must remember positions will be determined by the need that exists in any local situation. No position, except that of pastor, should be considered as being a permanent one. Should the need no longer exist, positions should be phased out and the personnel reassigned other tasks more in line with the needs of the church.

The Relationships to be Maintained

The ministry of the local church can be strengthened and extended because of an active church staff that maintains good relations with each other and that shares a common goal for the effectiveness of the work. It is also true that the ministry of a local church can be greatly hindered and even destroyed because of a staff that is divided in personal relationships and in mutual goals. There are some guidelines that will determine the effectiveness of a good church staff in their relationships with each other and the congregation at large. These guidelines fall into the following categories: (a) relationships with the pastor as the chief administrative officer of the local church; (b) relationships of the staff with each other; and (c) relationships with the congregation of the local church.

No staff can operate efficiently or effectively without someone in control and authorizing action, *i.e.*, the pastor. To have a staff of people operating without a chief administrator in an unorganized and haphazard fashion is to invite confusion. Every responsibility involves an accountability, and in the case of the church staff the accounting is to the pastor.

Staff members should be expected to fully inform the pastor concerning all activities and plans they have regarding their individual ministries. Although staff members may have their own ministries in a narrow sense of their own field, they are also responsible for the ministry as a whole and, therefore, need to keep in mind the total scope of Christian education. The pastor will see the entire ministry of the local church and will want to fit the plans and activities of one staff member into perspective with the other phases. It is the pastor's responsibility to see that the entire scope of Christian education activities of the local church moves along in a smooth flow of continual progress. He cannot perform his job well without being adequately informed by the members of the church staff. His responsibility for seeing the whole scope of Christian education in his local congregation may be illustrated along the line of staff positions. The following diagram depicts this concept:

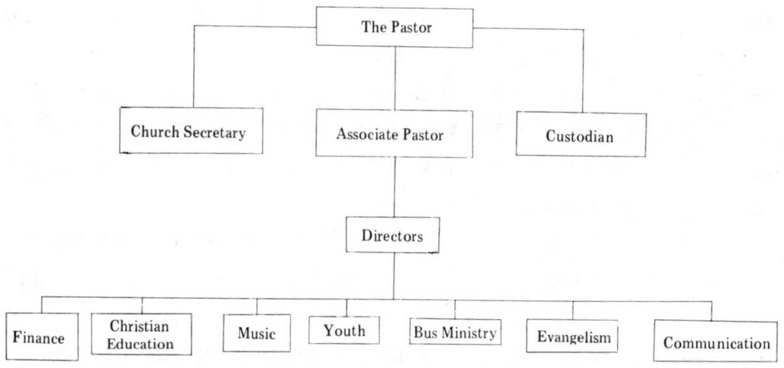

Naturally, this is not the only way the pastor views the scope of Christian education, but it is one very important manner of doing so. Furthermore, we must remember that each staff member, indeed each believer, needs to see the scope of Christian education as it relates to his or her particular responsibilities.

From time to time the pastor will find it necessary to issue specific orders to the staff. There will be things which he feels should be done in each area of the ministry and will, of course, require the person directing that area to alter his emphasis. The staff member is obligated to comply with the wishes of the pastor without hesitation or complaint. None of us should ever seek to be a member of a church staff if we cannot cooperate with the pastor.

There should be total support for the pastor among members of the staff. The pastor has a right to expect this support at all times, and the staff has a personal and professional obligation to give that support. There will be those within the congregation who will disagree with the pastor at times and will try to complain to a staff member or seek sympathy from him. At such times there is the opportunity presented to either undermine the pastor's ministry or to build it up. If the staff member determines that he cannot support the pastor's ministry, it is his Christian responsibility to submit his resignation. A church will be better off without any staff at all than it will if the staff works in opposition to the pastor, creating problems and division.

Seeing the pastor as the chief administrator is important, but it is likewise important to understand the relationships that should exist between staff members. For the effectiveness of any church staff will be in direct proportion to its unified thrust. There can be no lack of real cooperation between the various areas of ministry and the church still have a dynamic local church witness. For that reason members of a church staff have a responsibility to support each other and maintain the integrity of the whole witness of the church.

That responsibility includes a *mutual trust* that assumes each staff member is performing his duties in a professional, efficient, and Christian way. A lack of such trust tends to break down the lines of communication rather quickly. While an absence of this attitude opens the door for criticism, fault finding, and disagreement, the presence of mutual trust tends to build cooperation, quality, and desire into the minds and hearts of the staff.

Honesty and *integrity* also are involved in this responsibility. For Christians to do any less than what is their reasonable best in any endeavor is sinful. As it relates to full-time Christian work, for a staff member to be less than honest or to be careless in his work habits and personal life is catastrophic. The world at large tolerates sinful folk who are quilty of violating these principles, but the Christian worker will bring shame upon himself and all other Christian workers by such violations. A life of careful honesty and moral and professional integrity will enhance both the individual staff member and the workers at large.

Staff members should maintain careful *cooperation* with each other in the plans they make and in the activities they carry out. Conflicts in scheduling should be avoided by consulting with each other and by supporting the work done in each phase of the ministry. Some churches attain this cooperation by a daily or weekly staff conference in which all phases of the local ministry are discussed and all plans made for the future. It is this cooperation that will determine the degree of success for the local church in maintaining an active thrust into the community with the witness of the gospel.

In addition to having relationships with the pastor and each other, staff members have professional relations with the congregation as a whole. But for some, it is distracting to apply the term *professional* to the realm of Christian work. Using the word *professional* does not, however, imply a cold approach to our work or a purely materialistic interest on the part of the Christian worker. In relation to the church staff, it is meant to convey the thought of a high degree of competency and, thereby, confidence in the staff member by the people with whom the staff member may work.

Those holding staff positions in a local church should not

become depositories for rumors and gossip. Many have ruined any effectiveness for the Lord they may have had because they became known as busybodies in the church. The very nature of the work of the ministry will bring staff members into contact with many people every day. Some of them will want to confide in the staff member things that they would not tell anyone else. The integrity of the Christian worker will be reflected in the way such conversations are kept strictly confidential. Some of the people will want to pass on what they feel are facts that need to be known about other church members, or even other members of the church staff. The best policy is one of non-involvement in such rumors and a kind rebuke for those who would seek to draw the staff member into such involvement.

Many believers in the church will want to encourage a special relationship with members of the staff through personal favors, gifts, flattery, and compliments. The staff member will have to depend upon the Lord for an extra portion of spiritual discernment in such cases to know which people are motivated by a desire for personal gain in such things and which are not. The staff member should not go out of his way to encourage such treatment, or be in any way affected in his attitude of equal treatment to all members of the church. If special treatment is offered without any strings attached, the staff member should accept it graciously with thanks, remembering to ask the Lord to help him keep his own heart right in his attitude toward the giver. In like manner, there should be no resentment in the heart toward those who may not wish to extend special treatment to the staff member. If the Christian worker will not expect such treatment, there will be no disappointment when it does not come.

As the staff member moves among the members of the church, he must always remember his obligation, to the pastor, of sincere support. He can contribute toward the unity of the church and the effectiveness of the pastor's ministry by being always supportive of him. Some staff members have been guilty of building their own following of people in the church so that they can get their own ideas and programs across in business meetings. This is unethical, unprofessional, and, more precisely, unchristian. If the staff member has different ideas about things than those advocated by the pastor, let him tell the pastor and come to some agreement. No staff member ever has the right to promote his ideas in opposition to the pastor of the church among members of the congregation.

The personal contacts that are maintained among members of the congregation should always be used for the purpose of encouraging personal involvement and participation in the total program of the church. A part of the reward of Christian work is to see individuals grow in the Lord and become more useful in His work. Every contact should have a purpose, and every purpose should ultimately be to win the person to the Lord, encourage his spiritual growth, and help him to reach a level of spiritual development that reflects Christ in his everyday life.

Standards for Members of the Church Staff

When the local church reaches its decision to enlarge its staff to include other areas of ministry, it is faced with the problem of knowing what kind of person to look for in choosing the right individual for the job. There will be certain standards that are applicable only to individual church situations, but there are some general standards that will be true in all churches. The following standards are suggested for those churches seeking staff members that would increase their witness in the community.

As a first standard, we must look for evidence of a transformed Christian life. The potential staff member must be able to give account of his conversion experience through a personal testimony, relating the conditions, the time, and the place of his salvation. His life, too, must have been changed by this experience in terms of personal conduct, motives, values, and desires. If the candidate is not known locally, references should be required from those who have known the candidate long enough to give accurate and reliable testimony on his behalf.

A second standard is concerned with one's feeling a "call" to a specific area of Christian work or one's feeling that God has given him particular gifts for a certain ministry. Christian work is unique. It must not be approached simply with an attitude of earning a living. There must be a clear-cut indication that God has been involved in the decision to seek the work. A testimony of God's special calling should be asked for by those interviewing a candidate for a position.

Nothing is more of a hindrance to the work of the church than well-meaning people trying to fill responsibilities for which they are not qualified. Thus, the standard of acceptable performance must be enforced. If this is done, our churches will not be forced to lower their standards simply because we are involved in Christian work. The church should require references from those acquainted with the abilities of the candidate to determine his qualifications for the job.

Fourth, the candidate must agree with the doctrinal

position of the local church. To have a member of the staff advocating doctrines different from those held by the local congregation is to invite confusion and ultimately division. The candidate should be willing to be examined concerning his doctrinal position to assure the church of his personal beliefs. If there is serious disagreement, the candidate should not be employed by the church, no matter how well qualified he may be in other areas.

Additionally, the prospective staff member must possess a background of training, either by education or experience, for the job. The particular responsibility proposed for the staff position will determine what training is necessary. Formal education may not be necessary, but in our modern world it is becoming increasingly more desirable. The candidate must be willing to maintain his competency through a program of continuing education in his job responsibilities.

Finally, the candidate must be willing to work in harmony with the other members of the staff. It would be helpful for the candidate to meet the other members of the staff and have a time of fellowship to determine their compatibility. Nothing can be more harmful to the testimony of the church and to the effectiveness of the work than a staff divided among themselves. The candidate must be willing to do whatever is necessary to work in harmony with the entire staff for the good of the work as a whole.

Conclusion

As we review our emphasis in this chapter, several points become obvious. To begin with, we need to keep in mind that staff positions are in reality positions created by the gifts of the Holy Spirit. Moreover, these positions are to be filled by gifted believers who have matured to the degree that they have "crucified the flesh with the affections and lusts" (Galatians 5:24). This crucifixion includes, among other things, controlling feelings that may lead to "hatred, variance, emulations, wrath, strife, seditions, heresies (literally "factions"), envyings" (Galatians 5:20-21). Finally, we have observed that care needs to be given in the selection of any staff member. Carelessly chosen workers cannot be expected to reflect the qualities essential for the growth of a spiritually zealous, enthusiastic body of Christians. We must, in essence, select staff members in keeping with the spirit of Paul's admonition to Timothy: "Lay hands suddenly on no man . . ." (1 Timothy 5:22).

Discussion Questions

1. Do you think a formal staff as discussed by the author may be a hindrance to getting every adult Christian involved in the work of the church? If no, why not? If yes, can such be avoided?
2. Have you ever held a church staff position? Was the job description clear? Illustrate your answer.
3. What are some problems that are likely to arise out of staff positions that are multi-purposed? How can they be avoided?
4. Do you think a church would be wiser to limit full-time, paid staff positions or to maximize them? That is, would a church be wiser to hire one person to fill a position or develop several unpaid people to fulfill the same position? What makes you think so?

5. Does the fact that the staff should be loyal to the pastor necessarily mean the staff cannot openly disagree with him? If they may disagree, when, where, how, and why? If no, what makes you say so?

6. Does the statement that a staff member is obligated to comply with the wishes of the pastor "without hesitation or complaint" mean a staff member should never suggest an alternate way of doing things? Does loyalty to the pastor necessitate silence with him?

7. Does the author cover well the general standards of staff members? Would you add other standards? Would you clarify more the ones he has stated?

Chapter IX

The Organizations Of The Church

by Malcolm C. Fry

Introduction

The scope of Christian education involves many different truths, people, and institutions, but it also involves a large number of organizations. Our particular concern is with organizations at the local church level. Granted, the local church is an organism far more than it is an organization. Furthermore, may it ever be a living, pulsating, life-giving organism energized by the Holy Spirit of God! May we avoid becoming wrapped up in our organizations as many of the most influential churches of yesterday have done. To cite a cliche', however, we dare not "throw out the baby with the bath water." Organization, specifically within the local church, is both good and essential. Otherwise, the total church program may be likened to building a fence out of warped boards.

Do not the Scriptures say, "Let all things be done decently and in order" (1 Corinthians 14:40)? It is interesting to investigate God's orderly process in nature. For instance, each watermelon has an even number of stripes on the rind. Each orange has an even number of segments. Each stalk of wheat has an even number of grains. God is the master organizer; the universe is a vivid example of His handiwork.

So it is not surprising to find that the Scriptures contain many references to the use of organization. A classic example is the reference to Moses' division of the Hebrew people into groups of thousands, hundreds, fifties, and tens (Exodus 18:21-22). Every pastor can readily identify with Moses. Moses was serving as leader in every area of life in Israel; but on the advice of his father-in-law, Jethro, he divided the nation into groups and shared his leadership responsibility with other capable men.

The Nature of Good Organization

The Lord Jesus Christ reveals the importance of good organization in the New Testament. He chose the apostles and trained them to carry out His ministry. He sent out His disciples two by two. He told them what to do and asked them to report when they returned. This is a good lesson in organization; for with delegation of responsibility there must be accountability. Someone has aptly put it, "Responsibility can be spread but not shed." As the Lord Jesus Christ sent out the disciples, He delegated responsibility, gave authority, and asked for a report of achievement. Delegation comes easiest to the person who has a strong sense of the end result. He sees his objective clearly and strives to attain it through others while providing both guidance and leadership.

We need to ask ourselves how we personally feel about church organizations such as Sunday school, youth groups, women's groups, men's groups, training groups, and music organizations. Many people, especially ministers, have a negative feeling toward such enterprises and believe they only get in the way of a church's progress. Now it might be true that a church could be so overly organized that the purpose behind it would be lost in maintaining the organization. One leader in a large organization has stated that good organization is just as unnoticeable as the digestive system of the body when it is functioning properly. However, when one becomes aware of it, it means it is malfunctioning.[1]

On the positive side, when the church's work is organized, each person has a responsibility, and the responsibilities fit together to create teamwork. When organized properly, the groups pull together as a team. Much is achieved that could never be accomplished by people working separately. We ought to be candid; for we know that normally 80 percent of a church's work is done by 20 percent of its people. So when a proper organization takes place, the work of the church is distributed among a greater number of church members. This can provide an opportunity for the matching of skills or gifts of the Spirit with positions in organizations. Also, good organization enables us to identify our leaders. For instance, a training group sponsor understands that he is working under the guidance of the training director, and a Sunday school teacher understands that he is working under the guidance of the Sunday school superintendent.

Caution is needed, as good organization does not merely or simply happen. People must visualize the overall picture or scope of the organization. The only way all the members of an organization can work together as a team is for them to work toward the accomplishment of the same overall goal. It is pretty easy for a particular class or training group to become so occupied with its own goals that it loses sight of how it fits into a larger picture. Every opportunity should be utilized to emphasize overall objectives. Otherwise, we are apt to have a group that becomes so settled in a room that it refuses to move even when the space is needed more for another purpose. When such an attitude develops, it is a good sign that the unit has lost sight of the overall goals and objectives of the organization.

Every church should worship, fellowship, evangelize, edify, serve, and engage in acts of benevolence. The specific organizations needed for these functions may vary from church to church. Each church must study its situation and design the organization that best accomplishes its mission. All ministries must have a consciousness that they are working together at accomplishing their objectives. As a church identifies its goals and these are recognized and adhered to by all groups, results begin to be seen.[2] How a church organizes to perform its work is important. Either too much or too little organization can impair the church's progress toward its objectives. Let us now analyze the organization of the Sunday school in the light of our foregoing discussion.

The Sunday School

Since the main organization within the local church is the Sunday school, it should be seen as the church's primary Christian education instrument. Consequently, we devote considerably more time to it than we do to other church organizations. Our discussion will involve each of these ideas: a) the purpose of the Sunday school, b) the phases of the Sunday school, c) the organizational patterns of the Sunday school, d) the age groupings in the Sunday school, e) the leaders of the Sunday school, f) the curriculum of the Sunday school, and g) the standards of the Sunday school.

When we look at the purpose of the Sunday school, we see that it is to win unbelievers to Christ and to teach believers in the truths of God. One writer says that subsequent to conversion, the true function of the Sunday school is the fourfold development in an individual relative to the psychological, sociological, ethical, and religious/philosophical areas.[3] Another writer suggests that the purpose of the Sunday school is not only the conversion of pupils, which is the beginning of Christian education, but also the learning of important moral values.[4]

There is no questioning the fact that one of the supreme tasks of the Sunday school is winning people to the Lord Jesus Christ. Our job is to take children at the very threshold of life into the Cradle Roll Department. Our ministry continues by providing them with instruction and training through their preschool and primary years. Ultimately we intend to bring them into a saving relationship with Jesus Christ and then help them to bring their entire lives into harmony with God's will. In so doing, they will be Christian in all of the depth and richness that the term implies.

If we fail at this point in the local church, we utterly fail. There is little value in seeing our youth grow up with a knowledge of the Bible if they do not know by experience the Christ of the Bible. Let every avenue of Christian education proclaim this as its supreme goal: the youth about us shall be redeemed by the blood of the Lamb and brought into complete subjection and conformity to His will.[5]

In addition to this general purpose of the Sunday school, we can specifically say that the purpose of the Sunday school involves the following sub-purposes: a) teaching the Bible, b) training the mind and heart in eternal matters, c) developing the Christian character necessary to face victoriously life's problems, d) making each believer realize the necessity of preparing for the life beyond, e) teaching all believers to be examples in word and deed, f) encouraging each Christian to become involved in the Great Commission, and g) providing Biblical fellowship for Christians.

Understanding the purpose of the Sunday school is extremely important. Similarly, we need to be cognizant of the *four great phases* of the Sunday school. The administrative phase involves promotion, which is the function of the pastor, the Christian Education Committee, and the Sunday school general superintendent. It involves determining aims, establishing policies, and giving general oversight to the reaching of predetermined objectives. Every person in every home in our church community should be reached through a well-defined and delineated program of publicity and enlistment.

The educational phase is the function of the teaching staff. The teaching staff should be well-trained and encouraged to take refresher courses when available. A perpetual training program should be in existence in the local church for prospective teachers. The educational phase of the Sunday school, though separate and distinct from the administrative, complements it.

The teaching staff is involved in the evangelistic phase, too. The teacher's task is to lead pupils to a personal relationship with Jesus Christ, ultimately producing a mature disciple (2 Timothy 3:17). The Sunday school is responsible for presenting the way of salvation in understandable language to every student. Every Sunday school teacher is an evangelist whose greatest opportunity and responsibility is that of winning his pupils to Jesus Christ and helping them grow in the grace and knowledge of the Lord.

A Sunday school may have adequate space, a sufficient

number of classes, excellent teaching, attractive facilities, but without the visitation phase all these things will be short of complete success. The most important absentee to visit is the one who was absent the previous Sunday for the first time. This is the only way to prevent chronic absenteeism and to be sure that our "fruit . . . (will) remain" (John 15:16).

These four phases lead us to another crucial point: every Sunday school needs just enough organization to prevent confusion—and no more. The amount of organization needed will vary with each Sunday school. Organizational standards should never be law, but rather they should be guidelines. Goals should prayerfully be set for the Sunday school. The purpose of organization is to help in the accomplishment of goals by limiting the span of control of each worker. Goals should remain permanent, but flexible enough to allow for a change of plan whenever necessary. All staff workers should take part in establishing goals and develop ways and means to arrive at them.

Approximately a half dozen organizational patterns have been used by Sunday schools. We will discuss three of them. The first pattern is class oriented. In this pattern, there are no departments. The teacher of each class reports directly to the general superintendent. This type of organization is found usually in smaller churches where there are not enough classes in any one age group to comprise a department. The class-oriented pattern is pictured below:

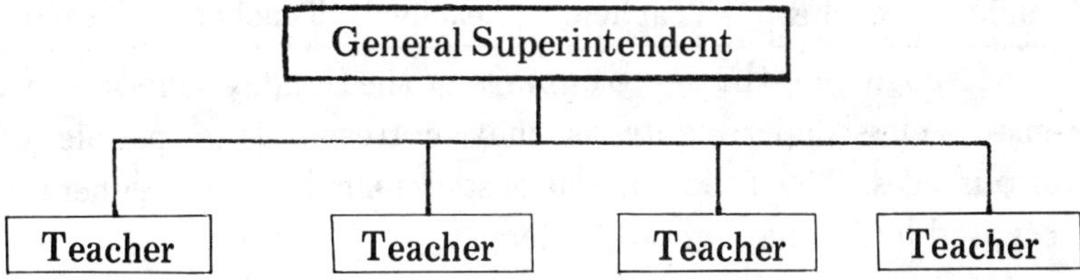

A second pattern is comprised of both classes and departments. Sufficient classes in some age levels may exist to create a department. Each department has a leader who supervises the teachers in that department. Each department leader is responsible to the general superintendent. Teachers in classes without departments report directly to the general superintendent. This kind of organization usually is maintained by the medium-sized churches. The ensuing diagram illustrates this approach:

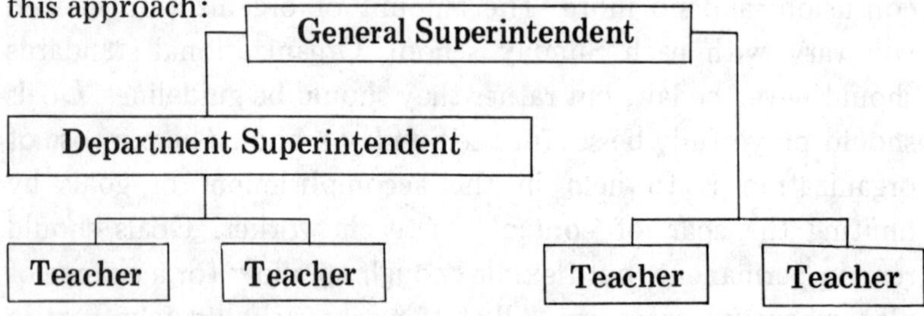

Larger churches may use the departmental pattern so that all classes in the church are grouped into departments. Each teacher reports to his departmental leader, and the leader in turn reports to the general superintendent. This pattern is diagrammed as follows:

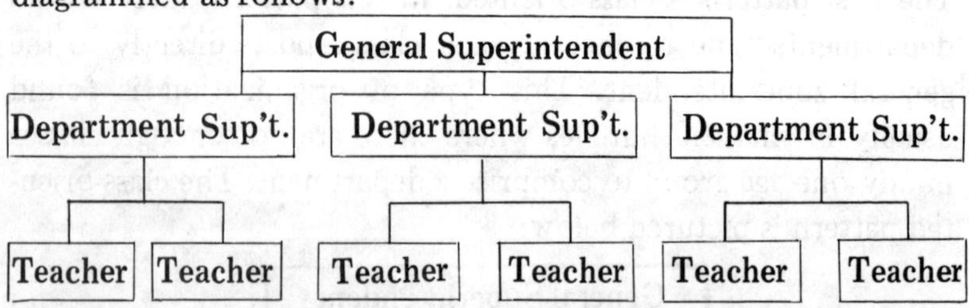

Recognizing the *age groupings* of the Sunday school is in a sense seeing departments as they correspond to people of various ages. The following suggested plan has been generally accepted by Sunday school leaders:

SUNDAY SCHOOL DEPARTMENTS	GRADES IN PUBLIC SCHOOL	AGES
Cradle Roll	-0-	Birth through 1
Nursery	-0-	2, 3
Kindergarten (Beginner)	Kindergarten	4, 5
Primary	1st, 2nd, 3rd	6, 7, 8
Junior	4th, 5th, 6th	9, 10, 11
Junior High (Intermediate)	7th, 8th, 9th (Jr. High)	12, 13, 14
Senior High	10th, 11th, 12th (Sr. High)	15, 16, 17
Young People	College/Career	18 to 24
Adult	-0-	25 and up

Individuals occupying *leadership roles* must be chosen carefully and trained thoroughly for their tasks with the previously discussed age groupings. An individual is done a great injustice when he is influenced to assume a responsibility for which he does not have a gift or the leadership of God. Most local churches and Sunday schools have clearly defined methods prescribed in their by-laws for electing officers and teachers.

Local needs and situations should determine the method used in identifying and electing leaders, *e.g.*, election or appointment. Regardless of what method is used, a specific plan should be utilized.

The most familiar leadership positions in the Sunday school include the general superintendent, the department superintendents, the general secretary, and the teachers. It is not our intention to cite specific duties and responsibilities of these leaders. Suffice it to say, the superintendents are administrators and educators; the general secretary is the statistician; and teachers are personalizers of God's Word to individual students.

Not only should we be concerned with the purpose, the phases, the patterns, the age groupings, and the leaders of a Sunday school, but we need to be interested in its *curriculum* also. The Sunday school curriculum should not only include precepts regarding salvation but also the fostering of a knowledge of Biblical principles applicable to daily living. The curriculum is the complete, prescribed outline of studies for a specific group of people. It is a means to an end in itself. It is used to guide to salvation and maturity in Christ.

The study of doctrine, church history, and ethics is regaining a place in Sunday schools. Some Sunday school teachers have become selective and prefer to use regular paperback books as texts instead of traditional Sunday school materials. Nevertheless, the Sunday school quarterly is making a comeback, according to a noted Sunday school expert.[6] There is renewed appreciation for systematically covering material rather than skipping around among topics that happen to be popular. The Sunday school curriculum is still the main part of the local church that provides a comprehensive coverage of the church's beliefs and practices.

Our final area of concern has to do with Sunday school *standards*. If we encourage the people of our churches to suggest standards, we will probably have a mammoth list. We can then refine this original list if we wish. If we use this approach, not only do we use the democratic process by involving all of our people in suggesting standards, but such action precludes a number of possible problems. After all, the guidelines will be the guidelines of the people themselves. Added to the list of several standards mentioned for staff members, we might find our people insisting that Sunday school workers be members of the local church, faithful attendants at services, and tithers.

Some church growth specialists suggest that the Sunday school could well be the barometer which predicts just what will happen to the growth of the church. In other words, if a Sunday school increases in attendance, a church can well anticipate growth. On the other hand, if the Sunday school attendance declines, a church can look forward to stunted growth and low church attendance.[7]

The Sunday school cannot possibly succeed unless it is well-organized and enthusiastically supported. Even a well-organized Sunday school, without constant attention, will drift and fall into a chaotic and disorganized condition. In order to protect and maintain a good organization, it will be necessary to preserve departmental lines, require regular reports from teachers and leaders, and conduct regular teachers' and workers' conferences.

Training Groups

The New Testament makes it clear that in a church there is no sharp distinction between "clergy" (the chosen) and "laity" (the people). There are differences of duties and abilities; but the total membership constitutes a "priesthood of believers," with every member responsible for witness and service. Effectiveness calls for training which will lead a person to put into action what he believes. A program of training for service is an essential function of every church true to the New Testament pattern. Several truths are apparent to those of us who are familiar with training in the church.

First, training is not a replacement for the Sunday school. It is a program for learning how to apply the truths learned in Bible study. The Bible teaching program of a church provides members with the Biblical foundations they need as disciples.

The church training program builds upon this foundation in guiding members to expand and develop all the skills they need for disciplined service. Every church needs a continual program of training for members, new members, and leaders.

Training is a priority item for the local church. It may well be a life or death matter for the church. The only way a church can have an effective education program, an outreach program, and a mission program is through an effective training program.

A second truth is that the organizational framework for a church training program could be similar to that for the Sunday school if training is provided for the entire family. A youth group may be a part of the training group, or separate, depending upon the desire of the local church. The training group may also provide areas of special interest relating to such areas as: a) teaching, b) ushering, c) soul-winning, and d) camping. Such training groups are a must for meeting specific needs within the local church.

Meaningful training begins when a person becomes involved in the church training program, whether he be a preschooler, a child, a youth, or an adult. It continues as he grows and matures. Though churches conduct training in age-division segments, each person experiences a single, continual process of training—a lifetime of training. Leaders in each age division should see their role as that of strengthening the spiritual foundation as well as building thereon.

Leadership training, as a third observation, from the New Testament church until today has been a secret of growing churches. For growing churches, recruiting and training leaders is important. The most effective training is firsthand experience. The pastor reproduces in a "Timothy" those qualities of life in Christ which are in turn reproduced in others. The pastor becomes the model. Both the recruiting and the training of leaders are the responsibility of the local church.

Finally, the values of a church training program are at least twofold. First, we see the value for the individual: (a) It will provide knowledge and understanding for responsible action as a Christian. (b) It will enable an individual to see and respond to needs in the lives of others. (c) It will build self-confidence in one's own ideals and values. Second, we see its value for a local church: (a) It provides trained leaders. (b) It develops disciples. (c) It multiplies the ministry of the pastor.

Without training for balanced growth of the Christian life and the development of people who can become leaders for the next generation, we will become totally concerned with either evangelism or worship. As good as both of these objectives are, neither possesses the whole truth and neither fits the historic image of a New Testament church.

The training to be done in the local church must really equip God's people for their ministry relative to evangelism, edification, worship, fellowship, service, and benevolence. It is imperative that the training offered be specific and not too general in approach.

We need a new vision of training in the local church. It should be a vision that helps us recognize that here is a wonderful opportunity for us to equip ourselves, to understand the gospel, to understand its relationship to others, and to understand the nature of the church and its ministry in a lost world.

Youth Groups

Youth are more open today than ever. They are searching for identity and truth. One of the greatest needs in youth work today is for spiritual reality coupled with practical training. We need to shape a ministry in the local church which meets them where they are and helps to lead them into wholesome Christian adulthood. A church youth ministry which fails to help teens "grow up in every way into Christ" (Ephesians 4:15) should be seriously questioned.

If we are going to accomplish this goal, youth ministry will have to be seen as more than youth "hour." The total ministry should include many activities, *e.g.*, regular meetings of the youth group, outreach and ministry projects. Often a week-long emphasis of involving youth in learning experiences can be offered so they can gain an understanding of their world, their church, and their community. Beyond the training hour, youth should be trained to understand their faith and also have the ability to communicate the reality of it to others within the church and beyond. A vital youth ministry should equip youth to live Christianity in their day-to-day experiences.

When we consider the subject of youth leaders, we have several options. Some groups have adult leaders only. On the other hand, there are groups with youth leaders only. A compromise between these alternatives seems best. Youth will develop their leadership potential with the help of adult examples, and adults need to work with youth to understand them. Two heads of different ages are better than one of any age. The adult could be called a sponsor, filling the roles of player-coach, and the young person could be the leader.

Youth sponsors must be everything and do everything they expect the youth to be and do. Moreover, they must see youth as individuals and not as a group. It is essential that sponsors talk little and listen much; be one *with* them, not trying to be one *of* them. Additionally, the sponsor must not equate activity with success, size with progress, presence with involvement, quietness with cooperation, noise with rebellion, and conformity with goodness.

The sponsor should guide the youth in his group into active participation, let them plan activities, be friendly and personally interested; but at the same time a mature adult to whom they can look for counsel. To make each effort doubly effective, the sponsor should work together with the Sunday school teachers.

Programming in the local church is an occasion for the sponsor to allow youth to emerge as decision-makers. In this way, the programs will be designed for the youth, not them for the programs.

Perhaps the primary task of the youth sponsor is not the dispensing of more information, but rather the personalizing of the information already received. Young people need principles by which they can live, rather than a program to entertain. Youth need to see that the Word of God has application to everyday affairs. The Bible tells of life—teens have to live; it tells of service—teens have to be active; it tells of joy and peace—teens seek satisfaction; it tells of the Lord and His salvation—teens demand security. The thrust in the local church should be to get teens into the Bible and the Bible into teens.

A meaningful and lasting youth ministry in the local church is built on basics and not changing times and fads. The lasting spiritual result produced in the lives of young people always comes from the solid building process in their lives. The foundation for such a process is the Word of God, not clever gimmicks or gadgets. Fun and fellowship are necessary, but the Word of God alone produces lasting results. The purpose of any youth program, then, must be to produce individual spiritual competence which can only come by a life that is solidly rooted in the soil of Holy Writ.

The challenge to the youth sponsor is to make truth the fantastically interesting subject that it really is, in order to combat the treacherous teachings of the cults and the superficiality of cultural fads. Poor theology and pathetic doctrine have characterized a tragically large segment of the gamut of youth programs and activities for Christians today.

It must be the object of the local church's youth ministry to build a proper understanding of Biblical principles and a correct method of applying them to the opportunities, problems, and philosophies of life. Any youth program should bring the many-sided possible Scriptural applications to the many-faceted problems of life. Confidence must be produced in the minds of young people that God's Word has within it the answers to the questions of what life is all about—though life may sometimes seem mysterious or appear to be hidden.

Sponsors and leaders have to plan activities to benefit their entire group if they are to be successful. Plans should have variety to stimulate interest and to prevent boredom. All major areas of the Christian life should be cultivated, not just the spiritual aspects. When plans are laid out and carried out, the former should be done by the sponsors and leaders and the latter by the youth as a group.

Young people love competition. Opportunities for Bible competition could be developed at various age or grade levels. For instance, a program of Bible Memorization could be designed for Grades 1 through 3; Bible Sword Drill for junior age, Grades 4 through 6; Bible Tic Tac Toe for junior high, Grades 7 through 9; and Bible Bowl for senior high, Grades 10 through 12.

Bible competition alone may isolate certain young people, so other areas of expression can be offered in the area of music and arts. Again such activities can be designed for the different grade levels to include creative art and creative writing, singing, playing an instrument, oral communication, and so forth.

Separate nights can be arranged for youth visitation and youth prayer meetings. Young people can take part in the local church's outreach ministry by assisting in visits to nursing homes, missions, juvenile detention homes, jails, and other special institutions. Also, they can be challenged to take part in tract distribution and church survey work.

Youth want to feel needed, and they are, contrary to a popular slogan, the church of today. Consequently, they should be provided opportunities for service in the local church: team teaching, ushers and usherettes, assistant teachers and leaders in Christian education, and filling various roles in the musical programs and ministry of the local church.

Operating hand in hand with the Sunday school and other agencies of the church—relating knowledge to the vital issues of life—will provide the youth an opportunity to put into practice all that has been faithfully taught. When they have been trained to do what they have learned, knowledge becomes habit. Habits form character and commitment. Young people will have, then, a clear-cut understanding of their faith because they have worked out the answers for themselves. Their understanding of God, essential Christian doctrines, and their own personalities and abilities enable them to share their faith with others in a meaningful way. Faith is no longer an abstract truth but a vital motivating force that guides them through purposeful childhood and adolescence into adulthood. Evangelism, edification, worship, fellowship, service, and benevolence become part and parcel of their everyday living!

Women's Groups

In a day of women's liberation, a women's group might meet with adverse reaction within the local church. It is encumbent upon the group's leadership, therefore, to properly present the purpose of the women's group in order to dispel any misgivings and/or misconceptions. For an organization for the women of the church can be most beneficial. A women's organization is not an *arm* of the church, as in the case of Sunday school, but serves in the capacity of an auxiliary. Still the local church's women's group should be considered a part of the total church program.

Consideration of the purpose of the women's group leads to the conclusion that it is not to be a fund raising group, a church cleaning crew, or a supper society. Positively speaking, it is an organization designed to assist each woman in the local church in the fulfilling of her place in the Great Commission. Likewise, it is an organization which allows many women to use their gifts of the Spirit to minister for the Lord Jesus Christ.

Specifically, a local church women's group should consider the following objectives: a) the strengthening of the spiritual life of its members, b) the developing of a genuine concern for those lost without Christ, c) the leading of its members into Christian witnessing, d) the magnifying of the Christian sharing her possessions, e) the cultivating of missionary convictions in the hearts of women.

When interest arises in organizing a women's group, prospects for the group can be gleaned from the church and Sunday school rolls. With the pastor's complete support and cooperation, interest in the organization can be stimulated by proper promotion, publicity, and personal contact with several of the women most likely to be interested and concerned.

The pastor's help should be obtained for the initial meeting. After the purpose of the organization is presented, action should be taken to officially organize, enroll charter members, elect a nominating committee, and set the time and place of the next meeting.

The monthly meetings should be designed to have definite objectives, and such ought to be spelled out so as to avoid misunderstandings. In this way, the meetings will not be thought of as gossip sessions.

After the purpose has been clarified and the group organized, the success of the organization depends largely upon the quality of its leadership. A good leader guides the energy and ability of a group into channels of activity which accomplish the group's purpose. In the women's group, every leader should possess the ensuing: a) the ability to work well with others, b) the willingness to assume responsibility, c) the skills to match the job requirement, d) a genuine concern for missions, e) a disciplined Christian life, and f) the desire to be loyal to the women's group program and purpose.

The following officers may be needed for proper functioning of a women's group. Specific duties can be outlined during an organizational meeting: president, vice-president, secretary-treasurer, mission prayer chairman, mission study chairman, and mission action chairman. A social chairman may also be desirable.

Programs for women's groups are usually centered around some materials published specifically for such meetings. Materials are readily available through denominational publishing houses as well as independent publishers. It might be wise for the women's group to design its program around at least three specific areas:

a) Mission prayer: intercessory prayer for missionaries, each other, and the local church. Special seasons of prayer and prayer retreats would add much to the members' Christian lives.
b) Mission study: in-depth studies of missions and mission personnel, constantly keeping the Great Commission before the members.
c) Mission action: Involvement should be the key as projects are carried out by the members for the lost and needy at home and abroad.

In every local church, there are places for women to occupy, and roles to be filled by them. A properly organized and functional women's group will do much to keep missions, mission-giving and causes before the entire congregation. Younger women in the church might be considered as a subgroup to the women's group. A special program for them would not only involve them in the ministry of the local church, but it can also be a way for the more mature Christian women to share practical aids for growing into a woman that is pleasing to God (Titus 2:3-5).

Men's Groups

Much of what has been said about the women's groups could be applied to similar groups for men in the local church. Men's groups have been in existence in churches for many years under such names as Laymen's Group, Brotherhood, Master's Men, Conquerors for Christ, and so forth. An active men's group can release the pastor from nonpastoral responsibilities, provide leadership for young people, render many services for the local church, and reap fruit in new converts.

Several objectives can be considered for adoption by a group of men, among which are: a) promotion of Christian fellowship; b) development of leadership for the local church; c) assistance in proclaiming the gospel of Christ; d) promotion of activities for boys that are Christ-centered; e) stimulation of benevolent acts in the church. Often a group of men becomes involved in conducting jail services, visiting in nursing homes, following a program of tract distribution, and meeting regularly for fellowship.

A suggested list of officers for a men's group is as follows: president, membership chairman, program chairman, activities chairman, song leader, and secretary-treasurer. Duties and responsibilities of elected officers could be developed by local groups unless otherwise specified in the local church's constitution and by-laws.

Ways and means of the men going beyond the local church may be considered by a men's group. For instance, a project could be developed to provide books for missionaries as well as the purchasing of books for the local church's library. The purpose of the first project would be to involve laymen in supporting missionaries with educational tools in up-to-date literature upon returning to the field. A second project could involve laymen in supporting missionaries with tools which would help them in building new churches and maintaining existing buildings.

A thriving men's organization in the local church will give trained leaders to all facets of the church; it will build fellowship among the men and will bring lost men to the church and to the Savior. Most churches do need men, but more than that most churches need to enlist the men they already have!

The Total Church Program

The need is greater today than ever for churches to possess a Christ-centered, Biblically-based, and Spirit-filled Christian education program. The social pressure of the public school which excludes God from its program and the subtle undermining of the Christian faith resulting from a secularized culture are tremendous forces driving people away from their Christian heritage.

Christian education in the local church involves more than Sunday school teaching. It is the "whole ball of wax," so to speak. T.C.P. was a very popular gasoline additive a few years ago, which was supposed to give new pep to cars. This acronym could also stand for *Total Church Program.* Christian education should permeate every phase of the local church program and ministry. The result would be the creation of new enthusiam and an increase in the interest and attendance in all the services of the church as well as a well-balanced program—a creation of unity and balance in the church activities.

Any vision for church growth must include the entire scope of Christian education in the local church: the Sunday school, women's group, men's group, youth groups, training groups. All organizations must have a consciousness that they are working together at winning people for Christ. As a church identifies its goals and these are accepted by all the groups, results begin to be seen.

It is essential that all the organizations of the church see themselves in a double light. For example, the women's group makes for good fellowship. The women get together, have a good time, come to know each other, and study the Bible. But the women's organization must not stop here. The women's organization, if properly understood, is also a means for reaching other women for Christ.

A church organizes itself to do its work. Most churches develop several organizations, such as those we have discussed, with specific assignments. These organizations have specific functions to perform which complement one another. There is considerable overlapping among the membership. To achieve the church's objectives most effectively, these organizations should coordinate their work into one harmonious program of work. The following illustrative diagram shows how the work of the local church may be seen as a whole:

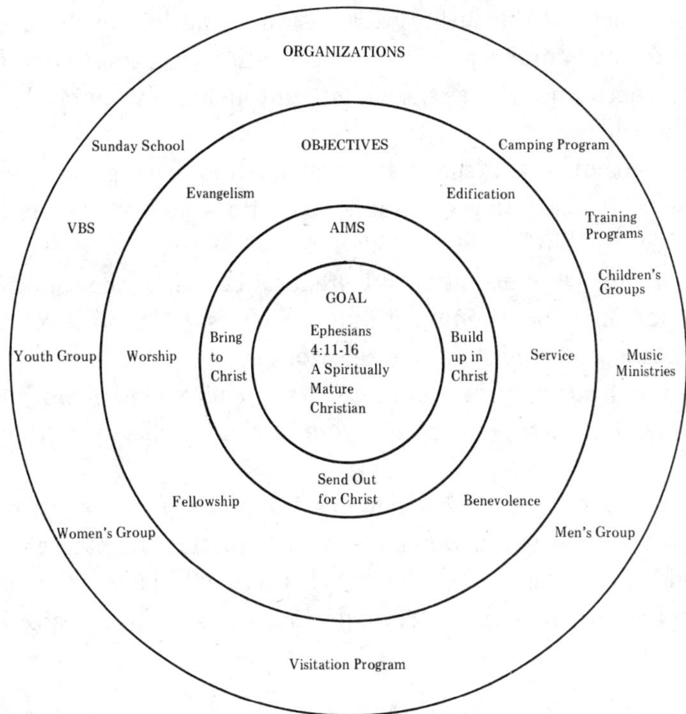

The church begins to coordinate the total church program as it develops the plans that are placed on the church calendar. Effective coordination, after all, is impossible without effective planning. All this brings us back to the starting point of local church organization, delegation of authority and responsibility, and follow-up through a Christian education committee or board to ensure the implementation and coordination of the total church program in carrying out the objectives of evangelism, edification, worship, fellowship, service, and benevolence.

Discussion Questions

1. In the light of the author's discussion, what do you think are the fundamental reasons for organizations in a local church? Are there important reasons left untouched by the author? If so, what are they?
2. The author says "the main organization within the local church is the Sunday school." Why does he say this? Is he correct? Why?
3. What are the essential differences between the Sunday school and the training group? What is your position on compulsory training for church workers?
4. Is it a healthy practice to separate church members into women's groups and men's groups? What makes you think so?
5. The author suggests that a men's group can greatly assist the pastor in his work. What are some practical recommendations that can be made in this realm? That is, what specifically can a men's group do that will assist the pastor in his work?

6. Do you think the purposes of the various groups mentioned by the author are desirable? Would you improve upon them in any way? If you would, how?
7. Some folks say that women are more interested in spiritual matters than men. If there is a difference of interest in spiritual matters, is such reflected in groups within the church?

Chapter X

Christian Institutions And Church Objectives

by J. D. O'Donnell

Introduction

One of the major facets of the scope of Christian education is that of institutions. Our present concern in this area is with a variety of educational institutions. Over the years we have developed many educational institutions to fulfill various functions in the Christian community. While all of the institutions we have developed have some functions that are directly related to the mission of the church, some of our institutions are only designed to indirectly strengthen the church in the attainment of its mission. We will examine samples of both types of institutions. In our examination, we will first seek to distinguish between the various educational institutions which serve the church. Later we will show how each of these institutions is related to the objectives of the church.

Distinguishing Features of Christian Institutions

The particular Christian institutions of interest to us at this time, of course, are educational in nature. Our list is not exhaustive but serves to point out the main Christian educational institutions related to the fulfillment of church objectives. With this limitation in mind, we will discuss now the distinguishing features of Christian day schools, Bible institutes, Bible colleges, liberal arts colleges, graduate schools, and seminaries. The following diagram depicts the scope of Christian education from this institutional viewpoint:

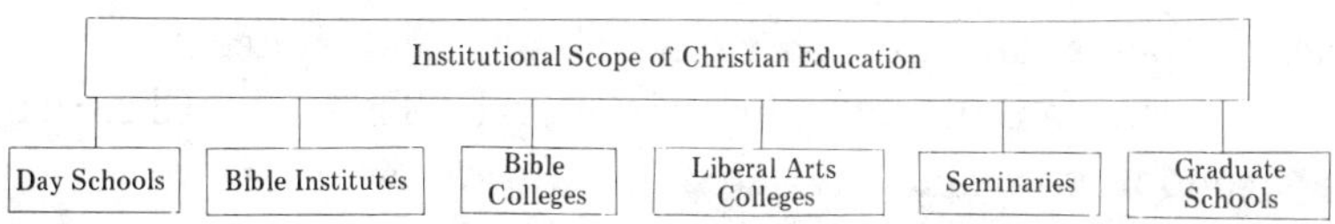

A wide-spread interest in *Christian day schools* is a rather recent occurrence among Protestant groups. Parochial schools for Roman Catholic children have been in vogue for years. Through the years the public school teachers had been of such a character that the average Protestant church felt relatively satisfied in sending its children to the public schools.

Several things happened in recent years to change the complexion of American society and to cause churches to begin building Christian day schools. A major force, but not the only one, that brought about the Christian day school movement was integration. Some people who disliked integration began forming schools to avoid it. Another major reason was the realization of the possibilities in such a private school system. The possibilities included not only dealing with non-Christian beliefs which had become prevalent in the public schools but also with the decaying moral situation in America.

Consequently, we now see a system of private, church-related day schools springing up across the land. These schools are offering education to children from kindergarten through the twelfth grade. Most of these institutions are endeavoring to offer the same curriculum as the public schools and many are attempting to meet state requirements for accreditation.

Christian day schools are trying to add other ingredients to the education of the youth. Besides providing learning in an environment which is more conducive to Christian growth, these schools are also providing classes that concentrate on Biblical instruction and Christian morals. Thus, the Christian day school is a church-related institution which is providing training for children and young people from the kindergarten level through high school.

A *Bible institute* is much more difficult to define than a Christian day school. The term has been used to describe a variety of situations. For example, there is the formal usage of the term to refer to schools like Moody Bible Institute which offer college level courses. However, when Moody was first named, it did not offer courses on the collegiate level. It has developed into this from a less refined academic situation.

The term *Bible institute* is also used to describe a special approach to meeting specific needs of a church or a group of churches. The courses offered run for a short period of time and usually offerings are limited to a narrow field. This kind of Bible institute is not permanent and is not intended to be perpetuated as a school.

A third definition of a Bible institute is probably to be found between these two concepts. This definition of Bible institute includes having a permanent setting, often related to a church or a group of churches. It offers a series of courses leading to a certificate or a non-academic degree. In this kind of institute, we find a sponsoring board and faculty. The faculty is usually part-time, generally serving also on the staff of the sponsoring church or churches. Student fees are generally kept low. Classes usually meet at night and only meet once or twice a week.

Perhaps the fundamental reason for organizing this kind of Bible institute is to furnish the local church or local churches with Christian workers. The training offered in such institutions, therefore, is strictly related to the work of the local church. The courses offered deal with doctrine, Bible subjects, church administration, and teaching techniques. Generally speaking, students do not have to meet any prior educational requirements to enroll. Though many may work toward a certificate, others may enroll just for help in certain areas of personal need. Oftentimes students who have a degree in general or technical training will attend to get religious instruction.

Churches in America have started hundreds of colleges and universities in America. These colleges in the beginning were usually structured basically to fill the need of the churches for workers, especially ministers. In time these colleges seem to have tended more toward general education, and the churches began to feel a need for schools that specialized in training particularly for church-related vocations. This gave rise to *Bible colleges*.

Another reason for the rise of Bible colleges was the time element. The older system of education required that a student attend a liberal arts college for four years before beginning his specialized training for the Christian vocation either in a seminary or graduate school program. To get the liberal arts degree plus a seminary or graduate school degree required a minimum of seven years. The Bible college program is designed to combine the necessary courses into an abbreviated curriculum of four years. This ensures getting workers to the field much faster. However, there is the disadvantage that the student reaches the field of service without the broader knowledge and skills that would be acquired in the longer program. Furthermore, there is the added disadvantage of having Christian workers who are often not as psychologically, socially, and spiritually mature as those who spend longer periods of time maturing and studying.

Bible colleges then are schools that are designed primarily to give training for students who are specifically planning to enter a church-related vocation. Studies other than missionary and pastoral training, however, have often been offered. For example, programs of study in music, teacher education, and nursing have been provided. The limitations set on Bible college programs seem to be more a result of the philosophy of the leaders of a Bible college than it does the definition of a Bible college *per se*. Accreditation by regional accrediting associations has been a secondary thing with many of these schools. Historically, only a few have sought it. Interest in regional accreditation, however, seems to be increasing. Many of them belong to the American Association of Bible Colleges. This association has helped raise the quality of the academic work in these colleges to a respectable academic level. The baccalaureate degree is the basic degree offered by Bible colleges. Many Bible colleges have a diploma of some sort to offer those who fulfill certain academic requirements but decide not to or cannot pursue the baccalaureate degree. This might be thought of as a type of Bible institute program within the college program.

A *liberal arts college* is one which is intended chiefly to provide general knowledge and to develop the general intellectual capacities of the student. This orientation stands in distinction to schools intended to supply the student with professional and vocational skills. In a liberal arts program, the student's mind is broadened by a rather extensive study of language, philosophy, history, literature, and similar disciplines. Perhaps it is worth noting, too, that many colleges are loosely called liberal arts colleges when in practice they offer degrees in the sciences and a number of professional fields.

Liberal arts colleges associated with churches or denominations usually make Bible and religious courses a vital element in their programs. Some church-related schools require all students to be enrolled in at least one Bible or religion course as long as they are enrolled or until they have met certain requirements.

Church-related liberal arts colleges should be thought of as colleges training students for all areas of life, not merely church vocations. The majority of students in most instances may be preparing for secular professions, but liberal arts colleges are also training those who will enter Christian ministries. The liberal arts program was not historically designed to prepare the student for his specific vocation. It was intended to develop his basic skills, and he was then expected to go to a graduate school or seminary for in-depth training that would prepare him for his particular vocation or profession. Today, however, there is an increasing interest in professional fields by many liberal arts institutions.

Graduate schools are usually extensions of the liberal arts college program. Whereas the liberal arts college gives the baccalaureate degree for attaining a level of general knowledge and the development of basic skills, the graduate school is designed to offer degrees in specialized fields. Usually the fields of specialization are not nearly so broad as the range of studies in the undergraduate program. In fact, many graduate schools offer degrees in a very limited number of fields. Some graduate schools sponsored by churches may offer a broad undergraduate program and then offer graduate work only in the field of religion. The offerings are generally broadened as the needs of the school's constituents are enlarged.

The degrees offered in a graduate school are usually the master of arts or master of science followed by the doctor of philosophy. Schools with specialties, such as education, might offer the doctorate degree in their field of specialization.

Usually a graduate school is related to a liberal arts college and the two together form a university. A university proper is made up of an undergraduate division which confers bachelor's degrees and a graduate division which comprises a graduate school and professional schools each of which may confer master's degrees and doctorates.

The purpose of a graduate school or a university is to furnish the highest degrees in the broadest fields of education. Though universities do tend to specialize or limit their fields of study, technically there is no limit to the range of studies to be encompassed in their programs.

The word *seminary* comes from a word meaning "seedbed." The term has been used to include many institutions formed to give secondary or higher education. For our purpose, the term will be used to describe those institutions set up for training of ministers, missionaries, church musicians, Christian education directors, Christian psychologists, and other candidates for church vocations. While the thrust of the graduate school program is broad and can cover all areas of education and training, the emphasis of the seminary is on training for church-related vocations. The seminary offers graduate degrees, both masters and doctors, but the fields of specialization are limited to training for service in the area of religion.

The seminary offers its training then beyond the baccalaureate degree. Seminaries desire that a student come to them already prepared in his undergraduate field by a broad based education. The seminary is set up to give him advanced training in his special vocation or profession.

If these institutions so desire, they can set themselves up to give training in the whole scope of education. From this standpoint, an ideal education program of an individual would advance from the day school, through a liberal arts college or a Bible college to a graduate school or seminary, depending upon his chosen profession or vocation. One who had been called as a minister upon graduation from a day school should attend either a liberal arts college or a Bible college before enrolling in a seminary. Or there might be a particular graduate school of religion that would offer the program which he desired. A person who did not feel that he could spend seven years or more beyond high school in preparation for the ministry should plan to enroll in the shorter program of a Bible college. A person planning on being an engineer should plan after high school to go to a liberal arts college and then to enter a graduate school to specialize in engineering. One planning to be a physician will, after completing prerequisites, enter a medical school, which is just another type of graduate school.

The Bible institute program serves in different situations. A person who did not finish his high school education would qualify to continue his training in a Bible institute. A person who had completed his professional training but who wanted to get training in some phase of service in his local church could get it in a Bible institute.

A further distinction might be made between the intent of seminary training and the training offered in a graduate school of religion. The graduate school has historically aimed at the training of professors and researchers while seminary has been concerned with training church workers. The graduates of the former would tend more to be specialists while the intent of the seminary is pointed more toward developing workers with broad practical interests and skills. However, these orientations are no longer as rigid as they once were.

Church Objectives of Christian Institutions

Every institution sponsored by churches should have objectives that parallel those of the churches sponsoring them. Any particular institution will not have the *exact* objectives of the church, for that then would constitute another church. The institutions which have been described differ in their relationship to the aims of the church, since the nature of these educational institutions is different from the nature of the church. Many times the objectives of some of these institutions will be broader than particular objectives of the church. For example, a day school teaches mathematics, science, and history, which would not come under the immediate objective of the church. However, the teaching of these subjects is indirectly designed to strengthen the mission of the church.

The church objectives which we will compare to those of the previously discussed institutions are as follows: evangelism, edification, worship, fellowship, benevolence, and service. In beginning it might be noted that the objectives of these institutions will be chiefly concerned with edification and service because of their nature as educational institutions. However, the other objectives of the church (evangelism, worship, and benevolence) will always be an indirect aim of these institutions.

The general education of most Christian youth has been left to the public school system. In recent years because of trends toward atheistic and evolutionary teaching in the public school system, Christian parents and churches have become alarmed and have formed *Christian day schools* for the general education of Christian youth. The basic purpose of these day schools is to take the place of public schools in the field of general education.

Day schools, nevertheless, have objectives that are closely related to church objectives. Christian day schools in general would require instruction in Biblical and religious subjects for the edification of Christian youth. This requirement would vary from school to school. Instruction in worship and actual participation in worship would also be a part of the activities in a day school. Christian fellowship between students and faculty would be a natural result of involvement in the school and would thereby attain an objective of the church.

Training for service would be an objective of a day school. However, this would more than likely be tied in with the general education of the student rather than being a specific objective. Actual service by the students would not generally be a specific objective of a day school but could result from other aspects of the day school program. Or, in some cases a Christian day school might, as a part of its Biblical studies, train students in serving Christ as witnesses.

The same thing might be said about evangelism. Although evangelism might not be intended as a specific objective of all

Christian day schools, as students enroll who are not professing Christians, they are evangelized by the faculty and Christian students. So it may be seen that most of the objectives of the church are in some way realized in a day school program. But the edification of the student through a program of general studies would be the basic objective. This edification would not be strictly limited to spiritual growth but to a total intellectual and personal growth.

The *Bible institute* would be almost singular in its objective. That objective would be edification. By teaching and training believers, its intent is to broaden the knowledge of Christian students and to enhance their ability to serve through training. Only Christians would be interested in enrolling in a Bible institute program, so evangelism among students would be unnecessary. In some Bible institutes, there might be a practical work department that emphasized evangelism and service. Thus, an institute's purpose would not be to evangelize its students but to motivate them to evangelize unbelievers. Though some fellowship would be involved in classes, actually it would be held to a minimum because of the type of schedules that most Bible institutes have and due to the limited contact among students.

The Bible institute is closely related to the objective of the church in edification. Actually it is just an extension of the work of the church in its teaching and training program. Whereas most churches maintain a teaching-training program for all its members, the Bible institute is maintained for those interested in broadening their knowledge and increasing their capacity for service. Many ministers are trained for the pastorate in Bible institutes. Usually these are men who do not have the background to enter a college program. Often they are men who have college work, but feel that the Bible institute will fill their need in Bible study. The Bible institute is an especially effective institution for training personnel who will be serving within the local area.

The objective of the church and the objective of the Bible institute closely parallel in this area of edification. It might be noted that the objective of the Bible institute does not extend beyond the immediate objective of the church as some other institutions do.

The objective of the *Bible college* is far broader than the objective of the Bible institute. The objective of the Bible college includes all the objectives of the Bible institute plus many more. The main objectives of the Bible college are edification and preparation for service. Whereas the Bible institute concentrates on preparing men and women for service in a local setting, the Bible college seeks to prepare them for worldwide ministries. In this sense the Bible college's objective is parallel to that of the church in fulfilling at least a major phase of the church's objective found in the Great Commission. Students are trained for the fulfillment of that commission.

Worship and fellowship are surely a part of the normal activities on a Bible college campus. But rather than being basic objectives of the college, they are furnished for the spiritual sustenance of the students as they are involved in the attainment of the college's main objective. Neither is evangelism a major objective of a Bible college. However, evangelism is a phase of the in-service training program of students. Almost every Bible college maintains a practical work department with a main thrust in evangelism and spiritual service.

The knowledge and training received in a Bible college for

the edification of the student are much broader than that received in the Bible institute. The fields of study are more extensive, and the depth of study in individual courses is much more intensive in the Bible college. The result would be a student prepared for a broader field of labor as well as a somewhat liberally educated graduate.

The objectives of *liberal arts colleges* are quite distinct from those of Bible colleges and Bible institutes. The main objective of these latter two institutions is the training and education of Christian workers for specific church-related vocations. While this can be one phase of the objective of a Christian liberal arts college and usually is, its main objective is to provide general knowledge and to develop the general intellectual capacity of Christian students regardless of their planned vocation in life. In this sense the liberal arts college has a different immediate objective than the church and an objective that is broader than the general objectives of the church.

Providing general knowledge to students and developing their general intellectual capacity as in a liberal arts college goes beyond the church's immediate objective, "teaching them to observe all things." The immediate teaching objective of the church is related to the gospel and the doctrine of the church. A Christian liberal arts school's purpose does not conflict with this and encompasses this to a certain extent. However, it goes far beyond this and is much broader.

While it is incongruous for a non-Christian to attend a Bible college or a Bible institute, it is not necessarily inappropriate for non-Christians to attend a Christian liberal arts college. It is out of keeping with the objectives of the former to try to train non-Christians for Christian vocations; it is not out of keeping with the objectives of the latter or of the church to give general education from the Christian viewpoint to students.

With this in mind, the Christian liberal arts college might have evangelism as one of its objectives. Since the college is serving the church, its Christian faculty and students would serve to evangelize unsaved students who enrolled in it. Worship and fellowship are usually provided for on the campus of a Christian liberal arts college, but these are not direct objectives. They are only provided for the spiritual benefit of the students and not as immediate objectives as in a church. Service and witness, as in the practical work department of a Bible college, are handled differently in many liberal arts colleges. They are required normally of Christian students or of those training for some specific Christian vocation. Service itself is not a specific objective of the college.

The objectives of *graduate schools* are as broad as those of Christian liberal arts colleges. In fact, they are parallel in most respects and are parallel to the objectives of the church in a fashion similar to liberal arts colleges. The objective of the graduate school is basically edification through the impartation of specialized knowledge in a particular field of study chosen by the student. Like the edification that occurs in liberal arts colleges, this edification is not strictly limited to spiritual or religious growth. It deals with the higher education or training of the student in his chosen vocation or profession. In the case of a graduate school of religion, the objectives of the institution are indeed parallel to the objectives of the church. However, if it were a graduate school of medicine or of law, the objectives go beyond the immediate objectives of the church. The objectives of the school of medicine or the school of law are broader than the objectives of the church, but those objectives do not conflict with those of the church.

As in the liberal arts college, the opportunity for worship and fellowship is provided, but these are not counted as immediate objectives in the graduate school. Also an opportunity for evangelism prevails if there are unsaved students, but neither is this an immediate objective of the graduate school. The same opportunity prevails wherever you have a body of Christians such as students and faculty.

The objectives of a *seminary* are parallel to the objectives of the church in the same sense as those of the Bible institute and the Bible college. As mentioned before in those relationships, it is incongruous for an unsaved person to seek an education in a seminary. The main objective of a seminary is to impart knowledge on religious subjects and to give practical training to those who intend to pursue church-related vocations. This type of edification is over and beyond the education that can be provided in the local church, but it is exactly parallel to the objectives of the church. Whereas the church provides its teaching and training for all members of the church, the seminary's task is to prepare those who had a special calling in some ministry of the church.

The seminary, like the Bible institute and Bible college, is performing a service of the church. As it trains Christian workers, it is serving the church in a vital work. The service rendered by a seminary aids the church in the meeting of its objectives. Though worship, fellowship, and evangelism are not immediate objectives of the seminary, the seminary is involved in the training of those workers who will ultimately be leaders in the church in attaining all of these objectives.

Conclusion

We have dealt with six educational institutions that are sponsored by churches—day schools, Bible institutes, Bible colleges, liberal arts colleges, graduate schools, and seminaries. These institutions play an important part in aiding the church as it fulfills its major objectives.

These institutions have been distinguished and the major objectives of each one have been noted. We have seen that most of these, because of their nature, have two chief objectives that parallel those of the church. These are edification and service. They are only incidentally concerned with worship, fellowship, benevolence, and evangelism.

Day schools, liberal arts colleges, and graduate schools have objectives that are much broader than those of the church (teaching science, mathematics, history, and so on). However, this broader scope of objectives is designed to strengthen the mission of the church. An educated Christian should be capable of rendering more effective Christian service.

Bible institutes, Bible colleges, and seminaries have objectives that more nearly parallel the objectives of the church. These indeed are involved in the edification of believers, but these are also involved in the service of the church.

The objectives of all these institutions have to be interpreted in light of their nature as educational institutions. They differ in nature from a church. For instance, the *immediate* objective of the church is evangelism. The *ultimate* objective of the seminary is evangelism. While seminary students should be involved in evangelism while they are students, that is because they are members of the church, and not just because they are enrolled in the seminary.

The product of all these institutions should be educated Christians who are better fitted to serve society through their vocations or professions in life. They should also be people who, by what they are, become effective witnesses for Christ.

Discussion Questions

1. The author mentions several reasons for the rise of Christian day schools. Which ones do you think are important? Why?
2. In the light of the author's description of the Bible college, would it be inappropriate for one to offer major fields of study in, for the sake of an illustration, philosophy, biology, mathematics, and psychology? Defend your answer.
3. If liberal arts colleges and graduate schools prepare most students for vocations outside of the church, why should the church support such? Why do you think so? Do the same arguments apply to Christian day schools?
4. If educational institutions do not have exactly the same objectives as the church, is it an ill-founded criticism that says such institutions are not carrying out the mission of the church? Why or why not?

5. If a church could only support one type of educational institution, which should it be? What makes you think so?
6. Which type of institution do you think is of least value to the Christian community? What grounds do you have for your opinion?
7. What is the author's concept of edification? How does it differ from the notion that is commonly used in Christian circles?

Chapter XI

The Challenge Of Christian Education

by Douglas J. Simpson

Introduction

In the foregoing chapters, we have concerned ourselves with a survey of some phases of the scope of Christian education. We looked at the educational practices of the Old and New Testaments, objectives of the church, role of the home, and responsibilities of the pastor. The staff, organizations, and institutions of the church were mentioned as well. The individual believer with his gifts was woven into the fabric of much that we touched upon.

Now the time has come for us to turn our attention to the challenge each gifted Christian has to become involved in Christian education. In particular, we want to examine some of the ways each believer can implement the ideas discussed in earlier chapters. We are concerned, therefore, that as individuals we actively pursue the challenge to serve Christ, especially at the local church level. Naturally there are other ways of applying the ideas we have already examined, but we selected this method since the local church is crucial to God's design for Christian education.

The approach we take to implementation is that of suggesting a model for encouraging Christians to become better involved in the objectives of the church. Our model is only an example of what may be helpful as each of us seeks to become effective servants of Christ. When we have developed into relatively mature Christians, this or some other model may well have become second nature to us. On the other hand, many mature Christians operate with a less structured approach to serving the Lord. Certainly the suggested model is not meant to be followed slavishly.

Our model consists of three steps. The first step is that of assessing our circumstances. Assessment is followed by the clarification of what we think our objectives ought to be. Finally, we move to the last step in this planning model, *i.e.*, making recommendations for our particular ministries. Once plans have been completed, we need to follow up our recommendations by actively doing what we have recommended.

Before we proceed to elaborate on these steps, it is important to respond to a couple of criticisms that are made against the model we will explain. First, a formal, structured evaluation and organization of life is distasteful to many people. Some who dislike structured evaluation argue that such stifles the Spirit of God and is too mechanical. No doubt form and organization may lead to the aforementioned errors, but it need not do so any more than structure does so in other aspects of church life, *e.g.*, Sunday school. Also the emphasis we may want to place on structure does not mean we should become mechanical. We still need to pray: "Search me, O God, and know my heart: try me, and know my thoughts: And see if there be any wicked way in me, and lead me in the way everlasting" (Psalm 139:23-24). The Spirit of God is essential in assessing our assets and liabilities, and He is just as essential in discerning which objectives to pursue and what recommendations to establish for ourselves. Thus, the entire process should in reality be a spiritual one.

Second, a formal, structured evaluation and organization

of our lives is unappetizing to many because of the time that is necessary to initiate the process and to maintain it. If we work together as groups of believers, the problem of time to construct forms for initiating the process can be partially overcome. The time needed for assessment of circumstances, clarification of objectives, and recommendations for ministry is not a significant amount. The actual time involved, in an intelligently functioning situation, would probably demand no more than a couple of hours each year. Those who, on the other hand, are obsessed with this approach or who think it is a cure-all for involvement in Christian education will waste many hours.

Assessment of Circumstances

The first step involves an assessment of our lives. This step is crucial because without an analysis of our present situation we cannot wisely proceed to later steps.

The integral elements of our lives that need to be evaluated will differ to the degree that we are unique people and have different gifts and responsibilities in life. Likewise, the manner in which we evaluate ourselves will depend partially on who we are, what we are doing, how much information we need, and how the Spirit leads us. Some folks will need to design questionnaires and gather information from a variety of sources. Others will need only to do some "armchair assessment" which will be followed by intentionally changing their lives to meet perceived needs. Regardless of how much information we need, the first step in our model for us as individuals—or as groups—is to make a list of the areas we wish to assess. If we know of a list used by someone else, we might adapt it for our purposes. We can, however, make our own list of broad categories that need to be evaluated.

For the sake of convenience, we will use the topics discussed in previous chapters. Our list, therefore, includes an understanding of the following: a) the Christian Scriptures, b) the church objectives, c) the spiritual gifts, d) the Christian home, e) the pastoral ministry, f) the church staff, g) the church organizations, and h) the Christian institutions. Even this short list illustrates that we will need to determine which areas will be evaluated first, second, and so forth.

Since an understanding of the Scriptures is needed by every Christian, we will illustrate what a so-called average church member might do in terms of assessment in this sphere. Our hypothetical church member may wish to rank his understanding of church doctrines and the books of the Bible on a scale of one to five. With one being the lowest rating, the numbers could represent a poor understanding, a fair understanding, an average understanding, a good understanding, and an excellent understanding.

Perhaps the simplest way to apply this concept would be to write out the doctrines and, then, record a number that best reflects our understanding. The average church member might, for instance, list the following doctrines and rate his understanding of them: a) doctrine of God, b) doctrine of Christ, c) doctrine of the Holy Spirit, d) doctrine of man, e) doctrine of angels, f) doctrine of Satan, g) doctrine of salvation, h) doctrine of the Scriptures, i) doctrine of the church, j) doctrine of last times. These doctrines, of course, can be further divided. The church member might also rate himself in the same manner with regard to the books of the Bible.

If a local church wished to assist its members—and such is advised at times—in the realm of assessment, a committee could design forms for each category that would be evaluated. A form to evaluate one's personal understanding of church doctrines might be similar to Form A. The questions on Form A are subjectively stated, not functionally worded. To take out some of the subjectivity, a checklist of sub-doctrines for each major category could be devised. This checklist could be attached to Form A. On the other hand, a functionally-oriented form could be developed to replace the subjective or impressionistic one we have.

Form A
PERSONAL ASSESSMENT FORM
Church Doctrines

Directions: This assessment form is for your personal benefit. Please encircle the word for each statement that best represents your present understanding of the specified doctrine. After you have completed this form, you may wish to consider ways of increasing your understanding of church doctrines, particularly in those areas where you rated yourself poor or fair.

A. My understanding of the doctrine of God is
    Poor   Fair   Average   Good   Excellent
B. My understanding of the doctrine of Christ is
    Poor   Fair   Average   Good   Excellent
C. My understanding of the doctrine of the Holy Spirit is
    Poor   Fair   Average   Good   Excellent
D. My understanding of the doctrine of man is
    Poor   Fair   Average   Good   Excellent

E. My understanding of the doctrine of angels is
    Poor   Fair   Average   Good   Excellent
F. My understanding of the doctrine of Satan is
    Poor   Fair   Average   Good   Excellent
G. My understanding of the doctrine of salvation is
    Poor   Fair   Average   Good   Excellent
H. My understanding of the doctrine of Scriptures is
    Poor   Fair   Average   Good   Excellent
I. My understanding of the doctrine of the church is
    Poor   Fair   Average   Good   Excellent
J. My understanding of the doctrine of last events is
    Poor   Fair   Average   Good   Excellent

Before a form like Form A is used, it will need to be explained to those who plan to assess themselves. A local church might use a comparable form to find out which areas ought to be stressed in special classes in the church.

Christians in various capacities need particular assessment questions or forms. Pastors, deacons, teachers, and other leaders who use a formal assessment approach need to make a set of questions for themselves or have someone design forms for them. At times *group assessment* will be helpful to congregations, families, staffs, teachers, and sponsors. A questionnaire intended to get a church's opinion of its major emphases may be helpful. Notice that the term *opinion* is used. Sometimes we may be more interested in observable *facts* than we are personal opinions, although facts and opinions need not be totally different. Form B, of course, only implies the kinds of opinions a church may be interested in collecting. Like Form A, this form will need to be interpreted for those who plan to assess a church's emphases. Terms such as *evangelism, maturity, fellowship, worship,* and *outside causes* may need to be discussed.

Form B
CHURCH ASSESSMENT FORM
Major Emphases

Directions: This assessment form is for the benefit of the pastor, church staff, and leaders of church organizations. Please rate the overall emphasis of the church on the items mentioned. Check the answer on the scale which you think most nearly describes the church's emphasis.

A. Our emphasis on evangelism is

    Inadequate   Satisfactory   Outstanding

B. Our emphasis on Christian maturity is

    Inadequate   Satisfactory   Outstanding

C. Our emphasis on fellowship is

    Inadequate   Satisfactory   Outstanding

D. Our emphasis on worship is

    Inadequate   Satisfactory   Outstanding

E. Our emphasis on Bible study is

    Inadequate   Satisfactory   Outstanding

F. Our emphasis on prayer is

    Inadequate   Satisfactory   Outstanding

G. Our emphasis on giving is

    Inadequate   Satisfactory   Outstanding

H. Our emphasis on outside causes is

    Inadequate   Satisfactory   Outstanding

I. Our emphasis on family life is

    Inadequate   Satisfactory   Outstanding

The concepts we have discussed show some possibilities for assessment. While each Christian needs to evaluate his or her own strengths and weaknesses, the same principle applies to families, organizations, groups, institutions, and agencies. Most of the time, assistance from a number of people will be extremely helpful in assessing our circumstances regardless of whether the circumstances are basically personal, familial, organizational, institutional, or otherwise.

Clarification of Objectives

After our average church member has assessed his affairs, he initiates the second step for becoming better involved in Christian education. This step is the clarification of objectives for himself as an individual. Incidentally, the same process applies to groups that need to clarify their objectives.

Objective clarification means that the person attempts to preserve his strengths while seeking to overcome any weaknesses. As he clarifies his objectives, he needs to keep in mind several principles. The first principle is that *we need to set realistic objectives for ourselves.* If, for example, our layman appraises himself in the area of spiritual gifts, he may use an assessment form much like Form C.

Form C
PERSONAL ASSESSMENT FORM
Spiritual Gifts

Directions: This assessment form is for your personal benefit. Please record your answer to each item in the space provided at the right. You are asked to rate your ability or interest in a number of tasks. Please be frank in answering. When you record answers of A and SA, you may wish to list an example of your interests and/or gifts.

> Legend: SA — if you *strongly agree* with the statement
> A — if you *agree* with the statement
> D — if you *disagree* with the statement
> SD — if you *strongly disagree* with the statement

Section I: Office Gifts

A. Evangelist: I am enthusiastic about presenting the gospel to people wherever the opportunity arises.   ________
Example:_______________________________________

B. Pastor: I am keenly interested in teaching and guiding people in their spiritual growth.   ________
Example: ___________________________________

Section II: Speaking Gifts

A. Prophecy: People think I am gifted when it comes to carefully explaining to others messages concerning guilt, judgment, and hope.   ________
Example: ___________________________________

B. Exhortation: People seem to be strengthened, encouraged, and comforted by my visits when they are experiencing difficult times.   ________
Example: ___________________________________

C. Teaching: People frequently comment on the clarity of my remarks about the Scriptures.   ________
Example: ___________________________________

D. Knowledge: People are often appreciative of the comments I
   share with them concerning the Scriptures.   ________
   Example: ____
E. Wisdom: People come to me to seek advice when they are
   faced with decisions.   ________
   Example: ____

Section III: Serving Gifts

A. Helps: God enables me to be very helpful in assisting others
   in their work.   ________
   Example: ____
B. Giving: God has blessed me so that I can joyfully give large
   portions of my earnings to His causes.   ________
   Example: ____
C. Faith: God has used me on occasions to trust him in new
   realms of service and in new endeavors.   ________
   Example: ____
D. Mercy: God makes it possible for me to feel deeply for those
   who are often ignored, criticized, or disliked by others.

                                                        ____

   Example: ____
E. Discernment: God has given me the ability to see dangerous
   doctrinal and ethical trends before others do.   ________

   Example: ____
F. Government: God makes it possible for me to eagerly
   coordinate and administer church affairs.   ________
   Example: ____

   Suppose our layman records either an A or SA answer for

items A, B, C, D, and F. Realism suggests that he will not be able to become *deeply* involved in all of these areas. Thus, he needs to prayerfully seek God's will as to which of these gifts to concentrate on using. Perhaps he should set as an objective being trained to teach a class. More than likely, though, he will not have the time to adequately teach a class of adults, counsel a group of teens, clean classrooms of the educational building, study issues of a theological and ethical nature, and direct the training sessions of the church.

Pause for a moment to notice that Form C is more appropriate for Christians who are already active in Christian education. For many Christians, a modified form designed to help them discover their interests and/or gifts would be more valuable. While interests do not necessarily indicate gifts of the Spirit, there is a possible connection (1 Timothy 3:1; 1 Corinthians 14:1). Discussion of this connection with those who plan to use the form would, therefore, be wise.

A second principle is that *our objectives need to be specific.* Instead of saying he wants to become more involved in evangelism, our layman is better advised to specify his objective by saying, "I intend to engage in evangelistic activities this year by visiting homes on Tuesday evenings." He would also be wiser to set as an objective obtaining a better understanding of Isaiah than he would saying a better understanding of the Bible.

Perhaps a word about the connection between assessment forms and objective clarification is in order. Earlier we noted when discussing Form A that a checklist of sub-doctrines for each major doctrinal category may be needed for explanatory purposes. For example, item B on Form A is concerned with a person's understanding of the doctrine of Christ. If, however, the person who uses a form similar to it is not aware of the sub-doctrines subsumed under this major category, he will not know how to evaluate himself nor how to set specific objectives, *e.g.*, whether he understands well the deity of Christ and if he should set as an objective studying Christ's deity. Consequently, assessment forms will need to be interpreted for those who use them or made more specific than Form A.

An additional guideline is that frequently—but not always—*our objectives should be stated in functional or observable terms*. Every objective cannot be stated in a manner which will allow us *to see what we are doing*, but this does not mean many of them cannot be. We cannot observe our meditating upon the Scriptures, but we can observe many other experiences. Rather than our layman saying, "I want to help my class grow in Christ," he might be better advised to set a series of objectives much like the following: "I want to see Ned and Helen control their outbursts of anger when they disagree on doctrinal matters." Instead of saying, "I want to get my pupils to love God more," it would be more functional to say, "I want to see my students' love for God grow to the point that they discard ________ and start ________."

A final principle to consider is that *our personal goals should be tied to statements of time*. We cannot dictate to God or others the precise time *they* must complete certain tasks, but we wisely can set deadlines for *ourselves*. Plans to *begin* activities as well as *finish* them may be of equal importance. Our layman who says, "By Thanksgiving I am going to understand our Sunday school organization," will have a built-in impetus to prompt him to reach his goal. We may have to revise our time schedules, but this is better than having no schedule. So, too, the church that plans to give ten thousand dollars to a Christian college is wiser to establish a deadline or a systematic method of giving (which implies a deadline) than to sporadically give to the institution.

These guidelines will serve us well if we are flexible in adapting them to our circumstances. They should not, however, be allowed to stymie either our unique, God-given styles of operating nor the immediate intervention of the Holy Spirit. If we allow them to so inhibit us, they become our masters, not our servants. Furthermore, we must guard against subtly coercing *everyone* to use the approach we are suggesting. Individual differences should be respected, and people should be allowed the freedom to prayerfully direct their lives without being intimidated by those of us who may use this method.

Recommendations for Ministry

We noted in Chapter IV that each Christian is to be a minister to other members of his or her local body of believers. Church leaders are to prepare the laity to be a self-developing group of Christians (Ephesians 4:11-16). More often than not, the ministries we recommend for ourselves should be established in keeping with the principles of stating our objectives. They ought to be realistic, specific, observable, and have a time limit.

How do we, however, establish our recommendations for ministry? Earlier when we examined the realm of assessment, we talked largely in terms of our *understanding* of certain fields. But assessment should include more than our understanding. It includes, as we implied in our introduction, support for and involvement in Christian education, too. While understanding is largely of a *personal* nature, support and involvement are predominantly of a *social* nature. Some of our recommendations, therefore, will be mainly private: a) studying the Book of 2 Timothy, b) meditating on the Psalms, c) praying for the Christians in Labrador. No sharp dichotomy between personal objectives and social ones exists, however. Praying for the believers in Labrador involves *supporting* others in their Christian endeavors. Yet, supporting and involving ourselves in Christian activities is still conceptually different from merely understanding. This being the situation, we need to assess our support for and involvement in Christian education. From this assessment, we establish objectives and, finally, make recommendations.

When making recommendations for himself, our imaginary layman may decide to enroll in a teacher-training program in his church, take a correspondence course, attend a nearby college, or study with his pastor. If he used an assessment form to evaluate his involvement in his local church's activities, he also can use it to set objectives and to make recommendations. Suppose he were to prayerfully answer the questions on Form D, asking the Holy Spirit to direct him as he responds to each item.

Form D
PERSONAL ASSESSMENT FORM
Church Involvement

Directions: This assessment form is for your personal benefit. Please check the appropriate answer for each of the following statements. Answers should be given in terms of what you believe God expects of you, not what someone else may expect of you.

1. I am satisfied with my involvement in the Bible study activities of my church.
   ________ Yes   ________ No   ________ Undecided
2. I make good use of the training sessions of my church.
   ________ Yes   ________ No   ________ Undecided
3. I contribute financially as I ought to my church.
   ________ Yes   ________ No   ________ Undecided
4. I attend services at my church as often as I should.
   ________ Yes   ________ No   ________ Undecided
5. I pray for the needs of my fellow Christians as frequently as I should.
   ________ Yes   ________ No   ________ Undecided
6. I enthusiastically participate in the outreach ministries of my church.
   ________ Yes   ________ No   ________ Undecided
7. I spend an appropriate amount of time preparing myself for my church responsibilities.
   ________ Yes   ________ No   ________ Undecided
8. I actively cultivate fellowship among the people of my church.
   ________ Yes   ________ No   ________ Undecided
9. I carefully make opportunities for my family to participate in special church activities.
   ________ Yes   ________ No   ________ Undecided
10. I regularly encourage my church to extend its ministry by supporting Christian enterprises outside of itself.
   ________ Yes   ________ No   ________ Undecided

Wherever our layman checks no or undecided, he has a potential objective and recommendation for himself. Imagine that his checks of no are on items 3, 6, and 8. Form E, a recommendation form, reflects one way he might choose to respond to his assessment findings.

Form E

PERSONAL RECOMMENDATION FORM

Church Involvement

Objectives	Recommendations	Dates
A. To increase the amount of my financial support for the church.	A-1. Give twelve percent of my earnings to the church.	A-1. Start immediately and continue on a monthly basis.
	A-2. Give anonymously three percent of my earnings to financially troubled people in the church.	A-2. Start immediately and continue on a monthly basis.
B. To involve myself on a regular basis in church outreach ministries.	B-1. Visit my absent students during the week.	B-1. Immediately and weekly.
	B-2. Volunteer for the Rest Home Team.	B-2. July 1.
C. To fellowship on a sustained basis with members of the church.	C-1. Invite my class to my home four times a year.	C-1. February 4, May 8, August 3, November 10.
	C-2. Respond positively to invitations from others to go to their homes.	C-2. As opportunities arise.

Many of us do not need forms of this sort to guide our involvement in our churches. If we do not, then we should continue to respond appropriately to the challenge we have to minister for Christ. Those of us who presently can be aided by this process may not need forms throughout our lives. Some of us might find the forms valuable as long as we live. Regardless of our needs, we ought to be alert not only to ourselves but to our local church members' needs in this realm. Providing for all of our needs, we can include the entire scope of believers as well as stimulate involvement in the whole scope of Christian education.

Conclusion

None of us is able to progress properly in Christ alone. We need each other's encouragement to mature in Christ, influence others wherever we are, and support those who pursue His mission. Consequently, intelligent, Spirit-directed planning by individuals, churches, families, organizations, and institutions is needed. The more we function as self-developing communities of Christians, the more successful we will be in going, baptizing, and teaching all peoples of the world. And ultimately the challenge for Christian education is for us to be and to give evidence for Christ "in Jerusalem, and in all Judaea, and in Samaria, and unto the uttermost part of the earth" (Acts 1:8).

Discussion Questions

1. How great is the danger of becoming "too professional and mechanical" in our responding to the challenge of Christian

education? Does the author adequately caution against the danger?

2. Do you think the "armchair approach" is better than a more formal type of assessment? If so, why? If not, why?

3. If you were making assessment forms for church members to evaluate the emphases of a pastor and a teacher, what items would you include? Develop the forms and then ask someone to comment on their appropriateness.

4. Would it be wise to have blank recommendation forms for church members? If so, what categories do you think the forms should contain?

5. Do you think that once a Christian becomes mature, he will need to assess himself? What makes you think so?

6. Can most Christians develop and serve as they should without the formal measures suggested in this chapter? If so, what procedures do you think ought to be followed by them?

7. What are some practical ways other than those mentioned by the author for churches to help individual members to assess themselves, set objectives, and make recommendations?

8. How often should Christians assess themselves in terms of the ideas indicated by the author? Should some people do so more often than others? Why?

9. Assuming that the "armchair approach" to assessment has merit, what are some of the guidelines we should observe if we use the approach. In other words, what can we do to provide some assurance that we will get beyond the armchair with our ideas?

FOOTNOTES

Chapter 2

[1]Clarence H. Benson, *A Popular History of Christian Education* (Chicago: Moody Press, 1943), p. 14.

[2]*The Complete Works of Flavius Josephus*, Translated from the original Greek by William Whiston, "Antiquities of the Jews," Book X, Chapters VII and VIII (Grand Rapids: Kregel Publications), pp. 32,33.

[3]J. M. Price, James H. Chapman, L. L. Carpenter, and W. Forbes Yarborough, *A Survey of Religious Education*, 2nd edition (New York: The Ronald Press, 1959), pp. 24, 25.

[4]Benson, *op, cit.*, pp. 23, 24.

[5]Frederick Eby and Charles Flinn Arrowood, *The History and Philosophy of Education Ancient and Medieval,* (New York: Prentice-Hall, Inc., 1940), pp. 141, 142.

[6]Frank Pierrepont Graves, *A Student's History of Education,* (New York: The Macmillian Company, 1954), pp. 23, 24.

[7]*The Complete Works of Josephus*, "Flavius Josephus Against Apion," Book II, p. 19.

Chapter 3

[1]C. B. Eavey, *The Art of Effective Teaching* (Grand Rapids, Michigan: Zondervan Publishing House, 1953), pp. 15, 16.

[2]*Ibid.*, p. 20.

[3]*Ibid.*, p. 25.

[4]*The International Standard Bible Encyclopedia*, Vols. II, V (Grand Rapids, Michigan: Wm. B. Eerdmans Publishing Company, 1960), Vol. II, pp. 904-05, Vol. V, p. 2923.

[5]*Ibid.*, Vol. V, p. 2922.

[6]*Ibid.*, Vol. II, p. 904.

[7]Eavey, *op. cit.*, p. 64.

[8]*Ibid.*, pp. 69, 70.

[9]Lois E. LeBar, *Education That Is Christian* (Westwood, New Jersey: Fleming H. Revell Company, 1953), pp. 49-86.

Chapter 4

[1]This translation is the author's and was done for this work.

[2]Same as above.

[3]Same as above.

Chapter 5

[1]For a more complete study of the nature of personal relationships see F. Leroy Forlines, *Systematics*, (Nashville: Randall House Publications, c. 1975), pp. 109-114; 182-187; and 190-192.

[2]Richard Chenevix Trench, *Synonyms of the New Testament*, (Grand Rapids: Associated Publishers and Authors, a reprint, n.d.), p. 356.

Chapter 6

[1]The research was done by the author for the M.A. degree from Anderson School of Theology, Anderson, Indiana.

[2]Gordon Allport, *The Individual and His Religion*, (New York: Macmillan Company, 1959), p. 39.

Chapter 9

[1]James L. Sullivan, "What Organization Can Do for a Church," *Church Administration* (October 1971), p. 42.

[2]Donald A. McGavran and Win Arn, *How to Grow a Church*, (Glendale: Regal, 1973), p. 67.

[3]Harrold D. Harrison, *Christian Education: The Total Task of the Church*, (Nashville: Randall House Publications, 1976), p. 14.

[4]Joe Bayly, "Sunday School—Expanding Structure Creatively," *Christianity Today* (August 6, 1976), p. 7.

[5]Malcolm C. Fry, *Discipling and Developing*, (Nashville: Randall House Publications, 1971), pp. 25, 26.

[6]Elmer Towns, "A Question of Purpose," *Christianity Today* (August 6, 1976), p. 8.

[7]McGavran and Arn, *op. cit.*, p. 66.